FOLLOWING JESUS

Catholic Spirituality for Adults

General Editor
Michael Leach

Other Books in the Series

Prayer by Joyce Rupp
Reconciliation by Robert Morneau
Holiness by William J. O'Malley
Diversity of Vocations by Marie Dennis
Eucharist by Robert Barron
Charity by Virgil Elizondo
Listening to God's Word by Alice Camille
Mary by Kathy Coffey
The Spirituality of Community by Adele J. Gonzalez

FOLLOWING JESUS

✳

John Shea

Maryknoll, New York 10545

Founded in 1970, Orbis Books endeavors to publish works that enlighten the mind, nourish the spirit, and challenge the conscience. The publishing arm of the Maryknoll Fathers and Brothers, Orbis seeks to explore the global dimensions of the Christian faith and mission, to invite dialogue with diverse cultures and religious traditions, and to serve the cause of reconciliation and peace. The books published reflect the views of their authors and do not represent the official position of the Maryknoll Society. To learn more about Maryknoll and Orbis Books, please visit our website at www.maryknollsociety.org.

Copyright © 2010 by John Shea.

Published by Orbis Books, Maryknoll, NY 10545-0302.

Manufactured in the United States of America.

Library of Congress Cataloging-in-Publication Data

Shea, John, 1941–
    Following Jesus / John Shea.
        p.   cm. – (Catholic spirituality for adults)
    ISBN 978-1-57075-721-1 (pbk.)
        1. Bible. N.T. Gospels–Criticism, interpretation, etc. 2. Spirituality–
    Catholic Church. I. Title.
    BS511.3.S535 2010
    226'.06–dc22

                                                        2009035096

For those who follow
For those who stumble
For those who get up

Contents

Introduction to Catholic Spirituality for Adults

C ATHOLIC SPIRITUALITY FOR ADULTS explores the deep-est dimension of spirituality, that place in the soul where faith meets understanding. When we reach that place we begin to see as if for the first time. We are like the blind man in the Gospel who could not believe his eyes: "And now I see!"

Catholicism is about seeing the good of God that is in front of our eyes, within us, and all around us. It is about learning to see Christ Jesus with the eyes of Christ Jesus, the Way, the Truth, and the Life.

Only when we *see* who we are as brothers and sisters of Christ and children of God can we begin to *be* like Jesus and walk in his Way. "As you think in your heart, so you are" (Prov. 23:7).

Catholic Spirituality for Adults is for those of us who want to make real, here and now, the words we once learned in school. It is designed to help us go beyond information to transformation. "When I was a child, I spoke as a child, I understood as a child, I thought as a child, but when I became an adult, I put away childish things" (1 Cor. 13:11).

The contributors to the series are the best Catholic authors writing today. We have asked them to explore the deepest dimension of their own faith and to share with us what they are learning to see. Topics covered range from prayer — "Be still, and know that I am God" (Ps. 46:10) — to our purpose in life — coming to know "that God has given us eternal life, and this life is in his Son" (1 John 5:11) — to simply getting through the day — "Put on compassion, kindness, humility, gentleness, and patience" (Col. 3:12).

Each book in this series reflects Christ's active and loving presence in the world. The authors celebrate our membership in the mystical body of Christ, help us to understand our spiritual unity with the entire family of God, and encourage us to express Christ's mission of love, peace, and reconciliation in our daily lives.

Catholic Spirituality for Adults is the fruit of a publishing partnership between Orbis Books, the publishing arm of the Catholic Foreign Mission Society of America (Maryknoll), and RCL Benziger, a leading provider of religious and family life education for all ages. This series is rooted in vital Catholic traditions and committed to a continuing standard of excellence.

Michael Leach
General Editor

Following Jesus:
Catholic + Spirituality + Adult

I PONDERED AND EXPERIMENTED with many ways of writing this book. What I finally decided on was influenced by the subtitle of the series: Catholic Spirituality for Adults. So I would like to introduce this book by reflecting on these three words.

Catholic

The Roman Catholic tradition has authoritative beliefs, stories, and practices that are meant to express and communicate its faith. This is the official rendition of the faith and it can be found, for example, in the *Catechism of the Catholic Church*. Individuals who enter the tradition are asked to understand and assent to the beliefs, listen and take to heart the stories, and attend and participate in the practices. As they do this, they will be socialized into the tradition or, in more religious language, they will undergo Catholic formation.

At the heart of the Catholic tradition are beliefs, stories, and practices about Jesus Christ. The beliefs concern his identity (Christology) and saving power (soteriology), and they emphasize the theological truths associated with Incarnation and Atonement. These beliefs have been forged in the fire of history. They came about to correct contrary beliefs that, in the judgment of the official Church, inadequately represented the reality of Jesus Christ. Some think these beliefs about Jesus Christ and their accompanying theological elaborations are the organizing center of Catholic faith. They influence all other beliefs either directly or indirectly. Beliefs about God, Trinity, Creation, Angels, Sin, Grace, Human Nature, Mary, Church, Salvation, Judgment, Afterlife, End of the World, Sacraments, etc. have been shaped, at least partially, in the light of the event of Jesus Christ.

The Catholic tradition also highlights the Gospel narratives about Jesus. "The fourfold Gospel holds a unique place in the Church, as is evident . . . in the surpassing attraction it has exercised on the saints of all times."[1] Although a theological argument could be made for the centrality of Gospels among the biblical books, the reason for the unique place of the Gospel narratives is that people who seek holiness with great effort and perseverance have always been attracted to them. A well-worn spiritual path is the imitation of Christ, which includes meditation on the stories of Jesus in the four Gospels. The Catholic tradition honors saints, and saints gravitate to the inspired stories of Jesus.

The Catholic tradition is well known for its many practices, and the most important and defining practices are the sacraments. In official Catholic thought Jesus Christ instituted the sacraments and is present and available in each of them. This rescues Jesus from being a past figure we remember and makes him a contemporary presence we experience. In particular, the Mass, with its Liturgy of the Word and Liturgy of the Eucharist, is the way believers continue to encounter Jesus Christ. As the *Catechism of the Catholic Church* states, "It is the mystery of Christ that the Church proclaims and celebrates in her liturgy so that the faithful may live from it and bear witness to it in the world" (no. 1068).

To be Catholic is to be part of both a tradition and a community.

Although many of these beliefs, stories, and practices are held to be divinely inspired and approved, they did not descend from the sky. They were developed by people who were responding to the concerns and challenges of their particular historical period. Therefore, underneath the creations of the tradition is the community, the people of faith who create, conserve, and change the tradition. To be Catholic is to be part of both a tradition and a community.

For our purposes in this book on following Jesus, there is one characteristic of the Catholic people that is important to emphasize. Some people of the tradition have understood and integrated the event of Jesus Christ into their lives better than others. Among those are the first followers of Jesus and, in later times, mystics, saints, and prophets. It is important to remember these people because they provide inspiration and lend credibility to our own efforts. They become guides, showing some of the twists and turns on the path of following Jesus.

But there are also the multitude of people who have walked behind Jesus and never made it into the liturgical calendar or were lifted up into the memory of the community. This is the destiny for most of us, and so these ancestors should be acknowledged, even if we do not know their names. We are not the first followers of Jesus nor will we be the last; and it is best to think of the followers of all ages and all places, the celebrated and the unknown, as one. Taken together, we are people who were shown the path, and — in one way or another and for some reason or another — we kept walking.

When we live within the Catholic tradition, we are continually directed to the mystery of Jesus Christ. The tradition has beliefs and theologies about Jesus Christ that it urges us to understand; sacred stories of Jesus Christ that it urges us to ponder; practices related to Jesus Christ that it urges us to engage in; people who are known as "other Christs" who it urges us to consult. When we accept this invitation into the revelation of Jesus Christ that the Church preserves and makes present, individual spiritualities emerge.

Spirituality

Spirituality takes the beliefs, stories, practices, and people of the Catholic tradition a next step. The tradition says belief in the Incarnation makes all life sacred; spirituality is how this belief changed Anne's consciousness and behavior. The tradition says that by meditating on Gospel stories believers put on the mind of Christ; spirituality is how by meditating on the birth narratives in the Gospel of Luke, Ron came to change his consciousness and behavior. The tradition says that through participation in the Mass believers become the body of Christ in the world; spirituality is how the experience of Eucharist changed Alice's decision about who she wanted to be with and what she wanted to do. The tradition has a calendar of saints who have followed Jesus; spirituality is how Jack was changed by reading Dag Hammarskjöld's *Markings* and pondering how a public servant was driven by a secret following of Christ. Spirituality focuses on the individual's journey of transformation through contact with the beliefs, stories, practices, and people of the tradition.

When we consider the "Catholic tradition" or "Catholic faith," we often do so in collective and objective terms. This is the faith of the Church. Its truth is based on revelation, tradition, reason, and the guidance of the Holy Spirit. All the faithful are called to espouse it in "a single voice." There is, if you will, a prescribed consciousness that everyone is supposed to have or aspire to.

However, as this objective and collective faith is engaged, an individual and personal process unfolds. The prescribed consciousness is reconfigured as it is translated into the actual consciousness of a specific person. Some Christological beliefs become more important than others and some theological elaborations of these beliefs become more relevant than others. Some Gospel stories of Jesus are preferred and others are neglected. Some practices, sacramental and otherwise, are lifelong companions, and others are engaged infrequently or not at all. While the faith of the Church in the mystery of Jesus Christ remains whole, entire, and intact, the spiritualities of individuals are mosaics, pieced together from selective and preferential contact with the rich array of beliefs, stories, practices, and people.

Therefore, we can appreciate the Jesus spirituality of individuals when they respond to two questions: (1) what are the beliefs, stories, practices, and people you consult to relate to the mystery of Jesus Christ? (2) how have these beliefs, stories, practices, and people influenced your consciousness and behavior? These questions are not easily answered. Individuals have to engage in reflective discernment and examine how their membership in the community of believers has personally affected them. What emerges may not be perfect or complete. But it will be authentic, an articulation of what really is rather than what should be.

Some think this emphasis on individual and personal spirituality is dangerously idiosyncratic. The beliefs, stories, and practices of individuals will abound with Christological errors and will eventually devolve into anything goes. Individual spirituality will speak to no one but the one speaking. To everyone else it will appear as an exercise in narcissism.

Therefore, it should be kept at a minimum and immediately corrected by guardians of orthodoxy.

Once an interest in spirit has been stirred up, people begin to look for ways to sustain and develop that interest.

However, this has not been my experience. When people tell their experience of the beliefs, stories, practices, and people they consult to relate to the mystery of Jesus Christ and how it has changed their thinking and acting, listeners and readers sense the seriousness of the adventure and begin the process of examining and developing their own spiritualities of Jesus. They ask questions that lead them into a fuller appreciation of the mystery of Jesus Christ and how it can transform human consciousness and behavior. What they are looking for is hard to define precisely, but it is easy to identify when it is happening. The Gospel of John calls it life and love, and individuals are willing, even eager, to pursue whatever communicates it. In this way, the sharing of individual spiritualities reshapes the community of faith to include "seeking" in its self-definition.

This emphasis on the distinctive way of each believer is why this book is entitled *Following Jesus*. Its original title was simply *Jesus*. But if we want a Catholic spirituality, we have to deal with the relationship between the faith of the Church and the individual's interaction with that faith. Both are needed and are intimately connected to one another. However, when we concentrate on spirituality, we focus on the twists and turns of the individual's journey, who we become and how life looks as we walk behind the long strides of Jesus.

Adult

Whatever else it means to be an adult, it means taking ownership for our life. In our times, many think "becoming intentional" is the hallmark of maturity. We pay attention and are proactive in regard to our physical and mental health, watching diet, exercise, stress, and scheduling regular medical exams. We pay attention and are proactive in regard to our work. We want positions where we will use our talents, where work and personal life will be balanced, where there will be adequate compensation, and where we will make a contribution to society. We pay attention and are proactive in regard to our relationships, making sure friendships do not crumble through neglect and commitments are kept with real enthusiasm and interest. And if, as always happens, events occur that were never planned or foreseen, we struggle to forge a response that is the best under the circumstances. It is our life and, even with the support of family, friends, and community, it is we who are responsible for it.

This adult way of paying attention and being proactive also applies to the spiritual dimension of life. We are not only physical, mental, and social beings; we are also spiritual beings. But spiritual traditions think the physical, social, and mental dimensions dominate consciousness. People are so wrapped up in the adventures of these dimensions that the spiritual does not appear on their radar screen. They are wide awake to bodies and relationships, but they are sound asleep to spirit. So when people become aware and interested in spirit, it is often called an "awakening."

There is a standard awakening scenario. Something happens that jolts consciousness out of its physical and social confinements. Since this could be almost anything, it is difficult to predict. But some of the experiences that are often mentioned are the birth of a child, the death of a parent or loved one, falling in love, recovery from a serious sickness, the loss of social position, a sudden and unexplainable depression, a recognition that one's religious upbringing wasn't all wrong, midlife questioning, etc. Some think that life eventually wakes up everybody to the reality and importance of spirit.

However, life itself cannot keep people awake. Once an interest in spirit has been stirred up, people begin to look for ways to sustain and develop that interest. They want more of what they have experienced. So the search begins. If they belong to a religious tradition, they may look for people who can impart its spiritual treasures. In contemporary culture where interfaith opportunities are readily available, they may dine at the table of a number of religious traditions. Also, there are many spiritual teachers from psychological traditions who are ready to give guidance. Awakened people become seekers; and, if their search is not successful, most likely they will fall back asleep.

One way of presenting the following of Jesus today is as a path of spiritual development for adults who have awakened to spirit. While it may include "churchgoing," it goes beyond faithful attendance and membership obligations. The Catholic tradition has many resources for the spiritually restless and hungry. The following of Jesus is today what it has been from the beginning — an invitation into spiritual transformation.

My Journey and This Book

I belong to that bridge generation who were formed by the multiple religious practices of pre–Vatican II American Catholicism and who had to reevaluate those practices in the years following the council. In my youth and young adulthood, I never missed Mass on Sunday; and since I was a seminarian, I also went to daily Mass. During the week, when I could not make the whole Mass, I received communion beforehand and made a mad dash to catch a bus for school. I went to confession weekly, prayed the rosary daily (well, almost daily), made visits to the Blessed Sacrament, said the Morning Offering and the Act of Contrition, was able to distinguish mortal and venial sin with scary precision, went to three churches on Holy Thursday, ended my Lenten fast and sacrifices at noon on Holy Saturday, sang too loudly and off-key during the Marian May procession, handed myself over to

God with a variety of night prayers, learned Altar Boy Latin, speculated on what the secret of Fatima was, had a decent respect for Lourdes water, etc.

I also heard and read the Gospel stories of Jesus over and over again. In fact, during my high school years I meditated on these stories with the help of a book called *Meditation Mechanics* (I kid you not), a simplified version of the Ignatian method.

When John XXIII opened the windows of the Church to let in a breath of fresh air, the wind ripped through these practices. Without going into detail, many of them were blown away. Some I deliberately stopped because I was no longer convinced of the theological positions that supported them. Other practices, and this may sound strange, deserted me. I did the practices regularly, and I wanted to continue them. But what once provided spiritual nurture now did nothing for me. My mind was not illumined, my will was not inspired, and my heart did not rejoice. I immediately blamed myself for this sudden staleness and redoubled my efforts. But eventually I could not dodge the evidence. I was hanging on to these practices out of a combination of obligation and nostalgia.

Then I came upon a remark attributed to the Buddha. "Once you cross the water, you no longer have to carry the canoe." I concluded, perhaps rationalized, that the practices had done everything they could for me. They had taught me how to navigate certain waters, but now it was portage time, an overland trip to more challenging waves. I buried many of the practices of my youth and young adulthood with honor.

Except for studying and meditating on the stories of Jesus.
I never abandoned the practice of meditating on the Gospels nor did the practice of meditating on the Gospels
abandon me. Of course, I changed how I did the meditation many times. I did not plan the changes and then argue
their merits. They were intuitive; it seemed the right thing to
do and I moved with it. I have written about the history of
these changes and the shape of my present practice in *Gospel
Light: Jesus Stories for Spiritual Consciousness* (Crossroad,
1997) and *The Spiritual Wisdom of the Gospels for Christians Preachers and Teachers: On Earth as It Is in Heaven*,
Year A (Liturgical Press, 2004). Part of this steadfast contact
with the Gospels might be attributable to the fact I was a
preacher and teacher and I used the Gospels in these ecclesial
tasks. My work demanded I stay in touch with the Bible. But
it was more than that. Meditating on the Gospels gave me life.
Although I am not able to completely explain it, my mind is
illumined even while it is being unburdened, my flaccid will
tightens, and my heart, believe it or not, laughs.

One major change in my meditation practice has affected
this book. I started to combine study and meditation. I had always studied theology and scripture, but I had not integrated
them completely, or even partially, into my prayer life. Now
when I am studying a text, I follow its lead into meditation;
and when I am meditating on a text, I will study it for greater
insight. This has considerably broadened my horizons and
given me a much better reflexive knowledge of my following
of Jesus.

Meditating on the Gospels gave me life. Although I am not able to completely explain it, my mind is illumined even while it is being unburdened, my flaccid will tightens, and my heart, believe it or not, laughs.

In hindsight, I realize my Gospel study and meditation was a way to steady myself during the Vatican II transition. I had returned to the origins to recover what was essential and should not be lost. But also I am acutely aware of the richness of the Christian revelation. Every articulation of it leaves a great deal on the cutting room floor. Even as I identified and retrieved what was important to me, I sensed other paths and possibilities. So this book describes only one spirituality of following Jesus. I present it in the spirit of dialogue with other ways in general and with the way of each reader in particular.

Overview

Over the last number of years, I have stylized the following of Jesus as learning to know and do the God–Self–Neighbor spiritual process. This is coded language, but it points to the spiritual process Jesus lived by and tried to teach to both his disciples and other people. We will explore how the Gospels present this process and what they think is required to learn it. But this is also a book about *contemporary* following, so we will explore how this Gospel process is supported and challenged by current knowledge. In particular, I will share some of my attempts to know and do the God–Self–Neighbor spiritual process.

A *contemporary* following has its distinctive challenges. These challenges come principally from two sources. The first is the default religious dramas that haunt the human condition. Whenever we become confused or afraid in following Jesus, we will be tempted to knee-jerk along the lines of conventional religiosity. It is difficult to pinpoint in advance what features of this drama will appeal to us. But the skeletal plot line goes something like: "God is an ultimate power who oversees life and whose primary abode is the transcendent realm of heaven. We struggle on earth trying to fend off destructive forces and enjoy life as long as we can. We petition God for help when we are threatened and for forgiveness when we have done wrong. God, in turn, keeps score and rewards and punishes both in this world and the next. The ways of reward and punishment are mysterious, but we can be sure they are just." This basic drama and its many spin-offs will not help us follow Jesus into the good news of divine-human liberation.

The second source of challenge is the cultural mood. We may choose to follow Jesus, but we have no choice about our culture. We are born into it, and whether we like it or not, we have internalized its assumptions. Some of these assumptions are friendly to the following of Jesus, but many are not. In fact, some of them question the whole undertaking. The project is ruled out before it has even begun. Can something that originated that long ago be relevant for today, even if it claims transhistorical truth?

Also, some of the specific instructions about following Jesus will run counter to contemporary sensibilities. Something like "cultivating dependency on God" mocks the cultural ideal of the autonomous self and seems to promote a prolonged childhood. So, in general, following Jesus into knowing and doing the God–Self–Neighbor spiritual process may not be immediately attractive or persuasive. We will have to argue for its intelligibility, relevance, and, most importantly, for its compatibility with full human development.

We may choose to follow Jesus, but we have no choice about our culture. We are born into it, and whether we like it or not, we have internalized its assumptions.

Our leitmotif text will be from the Gospel of John: "If you know these things, blessed are you if you do them" (John 13:17). This text is inserted after Jesus washes and dries the feet of his disciples and explains the meaning of this service. "These things" refers to the God–Self–Neighbor spiritual process. We have to know this process in a thorough and profound way. This penetrating knowledge will function as a precondition for doing it. But doing does not automatically flow from knowing. There is a chasm between them, and we must gain experience in crossing it. When we both know and do the God–Self–Neighbor process, blessing emerges.

As we learn to know and do "these things," we will have to pause and monitor each step. If we take a next step and do not know how it is connected to the previous step, we may go too fast. Although speed can give the impression of significantly advancing, it can also be a strategy for camouflaging the fact we have lost our way. Therefore, at the end of each chapter there is a section titled "Where We Are." This section recounts where we have been and where we are going. It is needed, for the following of Jesus has a justifiable reputation for being a hard road that leads through a narrow gate (Matt. 7:13–14).

Chapter One —————————————————————

Tracking Two Trajectories

L OOKING BACK at the Gospels from the vantage point of 2010, I see within these diverse yet unified stories the seeds of two trajectories. One is the Jesus trajectory. It is concerned with the saving power and identity of Jesus. The second is the disciple trajectory. It is concerned with what happens to people who choose to follow him. Both these trajectories are completely interwoven in the Gospels and in Christian tradition. In fact, some of the most creative reflection has developed the intrinsic and unbreakable connection between the truth about Jesus Christ and the proper religious and ethical responses of believers. Nevertheless the two trajectories can be distinguished and, for our purposes, the distinction provides clarity about why we are focusing on following Jesus.

The Jesus Trajectory

Jesus is an explosive and provocative presence in the opening scenes of Mark's Gospel. In one episode, he is preaching in the synagogue when a man with an unclean spirit suddenly confronts him (Mark 1:21–28). Synagogue theology advocated maintaining holiness by avoiding uncleanness. There were strict injunctions to stay away from certain animals, objects, and people. Even God needed [his] holiness protected from defilement. God was secluded in the inner sanctum of the temple, visited only once a year by the high priest, who had been scoured clean by ritual ablutions. However, there was a downside to shunning possessed people. It gave the unclean spirits free reign to demonize them. That is, until Jesus arrived.

The unclean spirit in the man, sensing a new and attacking spirit in Jesus, asks, "What have you to do with us, Jesus of Nazareth? Have you come to destroy us? I know who you are, the Holy One of God." The conventional answers to these questions would be that Jesus and unclean spirits have nothing to do with one another. Since Jesus is the Holy One of God, he would maintain this holiness by avoiding them. Jesus would go his holy way and unclean spirits would go their unholy way.

But there is an alternative, so startling and incredulous to the unclean spirit that it has to be phrased as a question, "Have you come to destroy us?" Jesus answers affirmatively with a thunderous command, "Shut up! Get out!" The unclean spirit comes out of the man. The people who witness this are stunned. "What is this? A new teaching — with authority. He commands even the unclean spirits and they obey him."

This is an example of Jesus' forceful and overwhelming presence, and it continues unabated throughout most of the

Gospel. Jesus forgives sin and a paralyzed man walks, he cures people and they return to their communities, he raises a dead girl and restores her to her parents, he teaches in such a way that he silences opponents, he instructs his followers with esoteric images and stories, he feeds multitudes in the desert where there is little food, he is transfigured on a mountaintop in the presence of three of his disciples, he predicts his future destiny, etc. Jesus walks through Jewish and Gentile lands displaying powers that are beyond ordinary human capacities. As both the religious elite and ordinary people take an interest in him, they move from attending to his words and deeds to asking a deeper question: "Who is he?" Readers of the Gospels know the answer to this question from the beginning. But for the people within the Gospel narratives, it is an ongoing puzzle that is never clear and is always open to debate.

This Gospel dynamic is a basic human way of proceeding. Mighty deeds precipitate the question of identity. When we see an extraordinary feat, we marvel. When we are done marveling, we wonder about the one who performed the marvel. This dynamic is expressed theologically as moving from the experience of Jesus' saving power (soteriology) to a confession of Jesus' identity (Christology). Therefore, Jesus is both Messiah, the bringer of salvation, and Son of God, God's presence on earth.

Over the years Christians have struggled to spell out this double conviction of Jesus as Lord (identity) and Savior (saving power). In the early centuries of the Church a guiding question was, "What think ye of the Christ?" "Christ," the title that translated Messiah and carried the conviction of Jesus' saving power, was assumed. What had to be thought out and affirmed was the underlying identity that made the Messianic power possible. What is the truth about Jesus Christ that has to be affirmed if our experience of salvation through him is to be credible?

However, once the identity of Jesus Christ was fully established, it became the primary truth, the first content of Christian avowal. The movement from experiencing the saving power of Jesus to affirming the identity that made that power possible was reversed. Now Christology, the identity of Jesus, was spelled out in great detail. In the process, it became logically obvious that he could exercise saving power. Therefore, the conclusion of one generation of Christians (Jesus as the Son of God) became the starting point of the next generation. But however the Gospel-inspired history of Christian concern with the identity and saving power of Jesus is told, it is a trajectory that never takes its eyes off Jesus.

The Disciple Trajectory

There is another precedent-setting episode early in the Gospel of Mark (Mark 4:35–41). Jesus and the disciples are crossing the lake when a great storm arises and threatens to capsize the boat. Jesus is asleep in the stern, on a cushion no less. The disciples wake him, accusing him of not caring that they are perishing. The awakened Jesus rebukes the wind and sea,

"Peace! Be still!" A dead calm replaces the storm. Jesus turns on the now-safe disciples. "Why are you afraid? Have you still no faith?" But, instead of answering these penetrating questions, they respond, "Who then is this, that even the wind and the sea obey him?" The disciples are interested in Jesus' identity; but Jesus is interested in their spiritual development. Fascination with the Jesus trajectory may have the side effect of overlooking the disciple trajectory.

Jesus fiercely states this possibility. "Not everyone who says to me, 'Lord, Lord,' will enter the kingdom of heaven, but only the one who does the will of my Father in heaven" (Matt. 7:21). Substituting belief in Jesus for personal transformation will not work. In fact, even if we prophesy in Jesus' name and do mighty deeds in this name, this may show we have neglected our own powers. And, on judgment day, Jesus will say, "I don't know you." Jesus recognizes people who have developed to the point where they can do what he does.

The poignancy of disciples trying to imitate Jesus is captured by the ambition of the chief disciple (Matt. 14:22–33).[2] Once again, the disciples are caught in a storm on a lake. They see Jesus coming toward them walking on waves. They think he is a ghost and are filled with fear. Ghosts are disembodied spirits who are known to haunt watery places and terrorize people. Jesus quickly corrects them, "Take heart! It is I, do not be afraid." Peter has a way to test if it is really Jesus. "If it is you, command me to come to you on the water." Peter knows Jesus gives away his powers. He is driven to show others how to do what he can do. If it is Jesus and not some ghost, he will teach Peter to conquer fear and walk on the waves.

Jesus simply says, "Come." Peter is out of the boat and walking on the waves toward Jesus. But he cannot keep his eyes on him. He notices the strong wind, begins to be afraid, starts to sink, and cries out, "Lord, save me." Jesus reaches out his hand and keeps him from drowning. He says to Peter, "You of little faith, why did you doubt?" Peter cannot hold his consciousness steady. His attention flits from Jesus' call to the danger of the storm. Captivated by its negative power, he begins to sink. In this peril, Peter, like most of us, forgets Jesus the teacher and calls out for Jesus the savior. Jesus, who sometimes acts in accordance with the way people name him, obliges.

But Jesus also forces the question: Why did Peter doubt? Why did his consciousness waver? Jesus does not know the answer to this question. It is an inquiry about Peter's consciousness, about what was going on in his mind that made him lose focus. As such, only Peter has access to the answer. He has to look inside and find the reason. Once the reason is found, he might be able to find ways to avoid it in the future. There will always be more storms and waves that need to be walked. The disciple trajectory is the way of self-knowledge and change. Development is paramount.

It is no secret that the disciples in the Gospels, especially in Mark, are not quick studies. Their inability to comprehend what Jesus is about and put it into practice is disconcerting.

Recently, I sat in a packed theater and watched an actor story-tell the entire Gospel of Mark. With great skill, he portrayed the disciples as rubes, chronically puzzled by what Jesus was saying and doing. They were alternately nonplussed, vocalizing their confusion, and then so blissfully ignorant they just went their merry way. Accompanying this benightedness was knee-jerk fear. They were always shaking in their sandals. The audience enjoyed this portrayal. It lightened up the story and got a lot of laughs.

I laughed along with the rest. But it made me revisit a question I have been asked many times. When I give talks on the Gospels to pastoral or educational groups and develop the theme of the nonunderstanding of the disciples, the predictable question is: "If the disciples knew Jesus personally and they didn't get it, what chance do we have?" My standard response is to sidestep the question and say something like: "The stories in the Gospel are written that way so that we can learn from the nonunderstanding and fear of the first disciples and be pointed in the right direction." The question was about the ability of ordinary people to understand and act in the way Jesus teaches. I pointed to the literary function of the stories that show us how not to do it. The question remains: Does Jesus walk too fast for ordinary mortals? Is he someone who should be worshiped but not followed? If the answer to these questions is yes, we have to revert to the Jesus trajectory, believing in his divine identity and power and opening ourselves to worship.

But as I was laughing at the portrayal of the first disciples, I wondered if I was laughing at myself. Am I really in a superior position to them because I get to observe their floundering? I am no stranger to nonunderstanding and fear, and, quite frankly, I have given up on ever eliminating them. So I began to formulate a humbler response to the question: If the disciples knew Jesus personally and they didn't get it, what chance do we have?

Following Jesus was a stretch for the first disciples, and it is still a stretch today. Jesus wants to pass on his way of thinking and acting to his disciples, but it is not easy for either the first disciples or us to receive it. So we should look at following him as ongoing spiritual development, combining experiences of both darkness and light. We should come to love the journey, a journey that has repentance at its heart. We will get it wrong and right, wrong and right, wrong and right. So, in a following marked by so much imperfection, why keep going?

Does Jesus walk too fast for ordinary mortals? Is he someone who should be worshiped but not followed?

I take encouragement from the most convoluted of Jesus' disciples, the first among equals, Peter. When many were "walking with Jesus no longer" and he asked the twelve, "Will you too go away?" Peter responded, "Lord, to whom shall we go? You have the words of eternal life" (John 6:66–69). Peter is right. We follow Jesus because we have a love of life, and we find the fullness of that love flowing from him. But I also fantasize that after Peter made this beautiful confession, he mumbled under his breath, "I don't understand these words of eternal life, but you have them."

Where We Are

Without any data whatsoever, I would venture that most Christians are more familiar and comfortable with the Jesus trajectory than with the disciple trajectory. We have multiple beliefs about Jesus' identity and saving power and the Magisterium's assurance that we should give our wholehearted assent to these beliefs. When these beliefs are understood at a deep enough level, they have implications for both our religious and our ethical behavior. This is clear, and it seems reasonable and doable.

At first blush, the disciple trajectory comes across as more individualistic and demanding. We have to go through community beliefs about Jesus and become personally familiar with the Gospel stories. We have to study and meditate on these stories in such a way that our consciousness and behavior is shaped by them. We have to engage in self-reflection to uncover both the thrill of following Jesus and our resistance to his instructions. This entails a number of skills. Some of them will have to be learned, and others are the standard stuff of any type of personal development. Also, most likely, there

will be a need for the support of a community of serious followers and the guidance of someone "who has been there for
a while" and knows the twists and turns of this less traveled
road. Looking at the disciple trajectory in this way, it appears
overwhelming, even forbidding.

Don't look at it in that way. There is a need to map out
what is entailed, but we should not allow the map to keep
us from taking the trip. Lawrence of Arabia has a section
in *Seven Pillars of Wisdom* about the night before you go
into the desert. As you look ahead, you envision everything
that could go wrong and wonder why you ever decided to do
this. But the next day when you are in the desert, two things
usually happen to your expectations. First, it is not as bad as
you imagined and you are doing fine. Second, it is as bad as
you imagined it, maybe even worse. But you find you develop
the skills and recruit the resources you need to deal with it.
Take a tip from Lawrence.

Chapter Two

Lodging the Word of God in the Heart

O FFHAND REMARKS sometimes jumpstart significant considerations.

Awhile back I was visiting my parents in Florida at the same time as my sister, her husband, and their son. It was early morning. I was sitting on the porch studying and meditating on a story of Jesus in the sight of a swaying palm tree — one of the best ways to hear the Word. There came a time when I realized I could not get closer to God until I had some coffee. I went inside and headed toward the kitchen.

My brother-in-law, who was a trader, had his charts spread over the dining room table.

"Market opens in an hour," he said. "I'm going to put some positions on."

"Go for it," I encouraged as I poured my coffee.

Back on the porch, the short exchange with my brother-in-law had lodged in my mind and was competing with the Jesus story for my attention. I remembered the Buddhist exchange about the student who complained to this teacher that the chirping of a bird was disturbing his meditation. The teacher responded, "Is your irritation disturbing the chirping of the bird?" Like many of the enigmatic stories of spiritual traditions, I almost know what that one is about. Obeying what I thought was its guidance, I decided to remember and ponder the words between my brother-in-law and myself. I suspected it wasn't a distraction but, in a way I had yet to discover, it was connected to what I was doing. The fact that it was holding on to my mind might mean it had something to say.

My brother-in-law and I were both preparing for the day. He was shaping a strategy he would shortly enact. I was meditating on the Gospels. His morning solitary preparation had a clear connection to his workday. In a boxing metaphor, when the bell rang, he would come out of his corner ready. How was my Gospel meditation connected to the upcoming day?

All prayer traditions deal with the relationship of prayer-time to non-prayer-time. The wisdom ranges from prayer-time is its own reward and punishment to prayer-time provides a God-consciousness that is the background for the events of the day, a background that under certain circumstances might become a foreground. Dietrich Bonhoeffer identified these two possibilities in concise and provocative language.[3]

Has it [daily prayer] transported her for a few short moments into a spiritual ecstasy that vanishes when everyday life returns, or has it lodged the Word of God so soberly and so deeply in her heart that it holds and strengthens her all day, impelling her to active love, to obedience, to good works? Only the day can decide.

Far be it from me to bad mouth a "few short moments . . . [of] spiritual ecstasy." In fact, I would stand in line with my hand out for any type of ecstasy. Consciousness is a moveable feast, and the fact that ecstasy vanishes into everyday chores doesn't bother me in the least. The alternation of heightened and flattened consciousness is just the way it is.

But "lodging the Word of God soberly and deeply in [the] heart" is definitely what I was trying to do on that Florida porch and, for that matter, in all the other places where I opened the Gospels. Another Buddhist story has an excited student gushing to his teacher, "Master, while I meditated, I had a vision of a golden Buddha." The teacher replied, "Keep meditating. It will pass." In developed spiritual traditions, prayer-highs are subordinated to consciousness transformation. I am in line with this. If it has to be an either-or, either highs in prayer-time or a consciousness significantly changed by the Word, then I will opt for the lodged Word of God. But as a Catholic, I always envision a both-and. I suspect spiritual ecstasy is the best way to lodge the Word of God in the heart.

According to Bonhoeffer, we will know the Word has been properly positioned when, during the day, it impels us to do good to others with such a force that we have to be obedient to it. This is active love, a caring response that is ever-at-the-ready. It is a going out of ourselves that is driven from within. From this point of view, my morning meditation on the Gospels was preparing my "within" so my actions would contribute to the good of the situations that the day would present. The ultimate goal of my study and meditation was attentive behavior that would benefit others. Therefore, from one perspective, my brother-in-law and I were not too far apart. We were engaged in formally similar activities.

Yet there are significant differences. His activity was a direct strategy to affect a market whose procedures he knew quite well. He was engaged in specific planning, mapping out the detailed tactics that he would later execute. I was not engaged in planning, in looking forward to upcoming situations and imagining possibilities. I was not even claiming virtues that I could reasonably surmise would be needed. "Remember, Jack, be patient and respectful to the students' questions." I was working on the spiritual dimension of myself, hoping it would have social effects later in the day. My brother-in-law was working directly on the social world of the market. Connecting the spiritual and social is a complex process and not as immediately relevant as devising strategies to intervene in identifiable situations.

This difficulty of connecting the spiritual relationship to God and the social relationship to neighbor contributes to the split in contemporary culture between spirituality and ethics. People talk about spiritual development in terms of awakening to their soul and discovering its grounding in God. It is a change in consciousness that broadens their horizons. But they can discuss this spirituality at great length without any consideration of how they act in the world. Becoming conscious of neglected areas of experience can radically alter attitudes and mood; and this is very desirable in itself. Why look any further?

On the other hand, people espouse ethical behaviors — values and actions — with force and persuasion. They take time to spell out in detail the personal and social implications of these actions. But they are slow to trace the grounding and inspiration for this way of living to the spiritual dimension. In fact, they often insist this does not have to be done. People can be perfectly ethical without any God connection. In contemporary culture spirituality and ethics often run on two different tracks.

However, the Gospels are adamant: this dual consciousness of the spiritual and the social must be cultivated in any following of Jesus. In fact, arguably, this is the main teaching of Jesus. So it is appropriate to study and meditate on the Gospels in order to connect God and neighbor because within the Gospels themselves this is the process disciples must learn. Two episodes in Luke show this process at work with particular power. The first is the skilled way Jesus uses the parable of the Good Samaritan to teach the lawyer how to do love of God and neighbor (Luke 10:25–37). The second is how Jesus lives out his own teaching under the pressure of his impending arrest, trial, and crucifixion (Luke 22:39–53).

Whatever It Takes

One of Jesus' most familiar parables is the Good Samaritan (Luke 10:25–37).[4] What is less familiar is that Jesus tells it to a lawyer who asks a specific question: "What must I do to inherit everlasting life?" Jesus returns his question with a question and asks him what the law says. He recites the double commandment of love. "You shall love the Lord your God with all your heart, and with all your soul, and with all your strength, and with all your mind; and your neighbor as yourself." Jesus tells him he is correct; and if he can do the double commandment, he will live. But it is precisely in the "doing" that the lawyer needs help.

The lawyer shares our concern. He wants to connect prayer-time (love of God) with day-time (love of neighbor), his spiritual life with his ethical life. Right now he can lay the two side by side, but he does not know how they interact. His knowledge is only on the informational level. Like many in religious traditions, he has access to the formulations of deeper wisdom, but he does not understand those formulations at a sufficient enough depth to enact them.

The lawyer thinks what will help him is a more precise definition of neighbor. So he asks Jesus, "Who is my neighbor?" He is looking to scale down the universe of people into some few who could be defined as his neighbor. This would clarify his obligation and help him learn how to do the double commandment. This is the totally wrong approach, and Jesus corrects it by telling him the story of the Good Samaritan. This story is a cameo of a man doing love of God and neighbor, holding together prayer-time and day-time, spirituality and ethics.

Prayer happens inside. Even if we watch people at prayer as Jesus' disciples watch him (Luke 11:1), we cannot spy directly on their consciousness. The only way we know what is happening on the inside is if people tell us or we deduce it from their behavior. Witnessing to our own interior prayer life is filled with problems, not the least of which is our inability to be congruent with what is actually happening in our consciousness. Therefore, the most reliable path is behavior. Prophets are known not by what they say but by what they do. The parable of the Good Samaritan is a complete action story, relating every detail of the Samaritan's behavior. We, and the lawyer, have to discern his interior consciousness from these actions.

The Lukan Jesus has criteria for looking at behavior and discerning interior consciousness. Specifically, there are behavioral indicators to show that a person is in communion with God on the inside.

> If you love those who love you, what grace is there in that? For even sinners love those who love them. If you do good to those who do good to you, what grace is there in that? For even sinners do the same. If you lend to those from whom you hope to receive, what grace is there in that? Even sinners lend to sinners, to receive as much again. (Luke 6:33–36)

Reciprocity is the normal human way. It is expected behavior, and therefore it cannot manifest interior grace, the love of God. Even people who by definition are out of touch with God, sinners, return favors. Then, what type of outer behavior can reveal an interior connection to God?

"Love our enemies, do good, and lend expecting nothing in return." What reveals love of God is behavior that goes beyond reciprocity, that cannot be explained by conventional motivation. These actions reflect the inner condition of grace. "You will be children of the Most High; for he is kind to the ungrateful and wicked. Be merciful, just as your Father is merciful." Human behavior that shows universal love imitates the universal love of God and reveals the acting person to be in communion with God. This is how love of God and love of neighbor are connected.

And this is precisely what we see in the Good Samaritan. He is an enemy of the robbed and beaten Jewish man by the side of the road. Yet when he saw him, "he had compassion and went to him." Where does this compassion come from? Since it goes beyond any common expectation like ethnic loyalty, its origins must be his inner communion with the Father of mercy. He is a child of the Most High. This communion with the source of mercy is further revealed in the abundant, creative, and persevering care he bestows on the person. "He went to him and bandaged his wounds, having poured oil and wine on them. Then he put him on his own animal, brought him to an inn, and took care of him. The next day he took out two denarii, gave them to the innkeeper, and said, 'Take care of him; and when I come back, I will repay you whatever more you spend.' " His "whatever it takes" attitude reveals the passionate excess of a loving God.

The parable was precipitated by the lawyer asking, "Who is my neighbor?" When Jesus finishes the story, he asks the lawyer, "Who proved neighbor to the man in need?" This reworking of the question is significant. The lawyer's phrasing assumed action is triggered by an outside person who qualifies as neighbor. If a person does not fall into that category, then no love need to be forthcoming. Jesus' phrasing shows action is triggered by the inner communion with God, which turns the Samaritan into a neighbor to all who live together under the "sun and the rain" (Matt. 5:45).

What reveals love of God is behavior that goes beyond reciprocity, that cannot be explained by conventional motivation.

The lawyer, Jesus, and the Good Samaritan provide some ideas about prayer-time and day-time, love of God and love of neighbor, spirituality and ethics. These ideas will have to be tested against our experience. Some will be more relevant than others.

- We may belong to a religious tradition whose major injunctions we can recite, but we may not understand them well enough to do them.

- Action should be distinguished from reaction. Reaction allows the outer world to dictate behavior. Action is a response from interior realities.

- The inner and outer dimensions of the acting person must be held together. Behaviors reveal interiority; and interiority eventually influences behaviors.

- Since acting persons can be aligned with God and allow God to influence their activity, it is enormously important how the relationship to God is understood and how the content of God's will is imagined.

- Actions inspired by grace are abundant, creative, and persevering.

- Compassion is a cognitive-affective movement that binds people to one another even if more conventional types of connection are missing.

There is a story by the Sufi master Attar of Nishapur that expresses the spirit of these learnings. Some Israelites reviled Jesus as he was walking through their part of town. But he answered by repeating prayers in their name. Someone asked him, "You prayed for these men, did you not feel incensed against them?" Jesus answered, "I could only spend of what I had in my purse."

"No More of This!"

At the beginning of the Gethsemane scene in Luke, Jesus, foreseeing the tumultuous and deadly events in Jerusalem, tells the disciples what is at stake (Luke 22:39–53).[5] "Pray, lest you enter into temptation." Prayer-time and day-time are explicitly held together. Prayer is the preparation for action; and the action, at least in the first moment, is resistance. This resistance is essentially the same as the petition of the Lord's Prayer: "Lead us not into temptation." We ask God to lead us in such a way that we do not succumb to temptation but are delivered from evil. The implication is that if we do not pray, temptation will seduce us, making us victims of its negative attraction and pulling us into contributing to evil.

Temptation is best understood in the spiritual categories of inner and outer. The outer world is always soliciting us to act on its terms. These terms may be good or bad; but when we categorize them as temptation, we discern them as bad. They want us to participate in them according to their negative dynamics. They have a purpose and a direction, and they will pull us along unless we have the strength to resist. Destructive forces that escalate and eventually take over situations always demand compliance. They want us to obey.

Although the disciples do not heed Jesus' warning, Jesus takes his own advice. He kneels upon the earth and begins to pray. "Father, if you are willing, remove this cup from me; yet, not my will but yours be done." These words also echo the Lord's Prayer, "Your will be done." But the human, heart-felt side of this petition is that it can conflict with what we want done. Jesus looks ahead and sees the inevitable conflict with the religious and political authorities; and he knows how these powerful forces deal with their irritations. He does not want to suffer, and he prays to God not to let this happen. Surely, this is the prayer of everyone looking into a future of possible pain and death. There is no glory in suffering, and no one should seek it.

But Jesus loves something more than he fears suffering. He is thoroughly committed to the divine will. Contrary to the sadistic strains in some Christian spirituality, God's will is not that Jesus suffers and dies. God's will is that the invitation to forgiveness and reconciliation be continued in all circumstances. This is what Jesus has pledged to do. In the events that will unfold, Jesus will remain steadfast to that commitment. He will never succumb to the violence of the outer world when it seeks to have him imitate it. He will forgive his persecutors (Luke 23:34) and offer paradise to the repentant thief (Luke 23:43). The reason he can do this is that his prayer life keeps him aware of God as the spiritual center from which his actions flow.

Jesus has spent his whole life giving people ears to hear; he is not about to start hacking them off.

Jesus' prayer is answered by the appearance of an angel. The purpose of the angel is to give him strength. Praying in preparation to resist is not about help in making the right decision. It is an intense process of inner resolve, a strenuous increase of attention and commitment. That is why Jesus is in agony. He is about to enter a contest and, the angel, in a way analogous to masseuses who prepare athletes to compete in the games, assists him. Athletes sweat water, but Jesus sweats blood, a symbol both of the violence he must resist doing and the violence that will be done to him.

When Jesus rises from prayer, the arresting crowd arrives and he confronts the hypocrisy of both Judas and the religious elites. But his major action is correcting the disciples' use of violence. The disciples have not stayed awake and prayed. So they engage in a preemptive strike. Violence has not yet arrived, but they see it coming and so they begin it. They ask Jesus if they should strike with the sword, but they do not wait for an answer. Instead, they use the sword and sever the ear of the slave of the high priest.

This is a symbolic cut. The beginning of violence is the end of dialogue. Once we start to fight, we no longer have ears to hear each other. Down to this day, we have to cease fighting to have peace talks which, when they fail, lead to the resumption of violence. Jesus has spent his whole life giving people ears to hear; he is not about to start hacking them off. His simple yet profound words, "No more of this," are followed by the action of restoring the man's ear. Jesus' prayer-time gives him not only the power to say "no" but the energy to forge a new and unforeseen "yes."

This episode also provides ideas about the relationship of prayer-time and day-time, loving God and neighbor, spirituality and ethics. Once again, these ideas will have to be tested against our experience. Some will prove to be more relevant than others.

- Resisting destructive situations is a major Christian behavior and always part of embodying the "will of the Father."

- Prayer-time does more than illumine the mind. It strengthens the will, and this entails strenuous inner work that deepens our commitment.

- If the goals of forgiveness and reconciliation are to be achieved, commitment to them must be reinforced because their opposites, retaliation and division, are so powerfully entrenched in the human condition.

- Once again, the formal process of opening to the Father must be accompanied by a keen discernment of the content of the will of the Father.

- When we go along with the escalating destructiveness of a situation, it is because we have not studied and prayed or cannot "hold fast" to the higher consciousness of our spiritual center.

- Resistance often brings about more persecution.

- Resistance to one way of acting should be complemented by showing another way of acting.

Gethsemane is only the beginning of the arrest, trial, crucifixion, burial, and resurrection of Jesus. However, it reveals the basic orientation that will sustain Jesus. This example of Jesus' inner prayer and outer resistance in the Garden sows the seeds for how Christians eventually would interpret his sufferings. "He committed no sin, and no deceit was found in his mouth. When he was abused, he did not return abuse; when he suffered, he did not threaten, but entrusted himself to the one who judges justly. He himself bore our sins in his body on the cross, so that, free from sins, we might live for righteousness: by his wounds you have been healed" (1 Pet. 2:22–24).

Where We Are

The premier practice of the following of Jesus is to study and meditate on the accounts of his life in the four Gospels. When we do this in a morning study/meditation/prayer-time, the question naturally arises how this affects the rest of the day. The answer is: through study, meditation, and prayer the Word of God is lodged in our heart and influences how we act in the situations that unfold during the day. The spirituality of the morning results in the ethics of the day. The relationship to God in prayer-time is woven into the relationship with neighbor in day-time. We are learning to know and do the God–Self–Neighbor spiritual process.

This contemporary activity continues the basic teaching of Jesus in the Gospels, a teaching he tries to impart to the lawyer through the use of the Good Samaritan parable and a teaching he personally lives out in the prayer and conflict experiences in the Garden of Gethsemane. These two pictures give us an initial understanding of the God–Self–Neighbor spiritual process. We watch the Samaritan love his neighbor with extraordinary behavior. We do not see his relationship to God;

we have to deduce the inner state that can support and energize these abundant, creative, and persevering actions. The most accurate estimate is that he is loving God with all his mind, heart, soul, and strength. In Gethsemane we see Jesus in prayer-time and day-time. We overhear how he struggles at prayer and then we watch him resist violence. Both these pictures generate ideas that help us.

We now have a basic outline of the God–Self–Neighbor spiritual process. However, in order to do the process, each part will have to be understood at greater depth. But, first, we should pause and check out our interest. If there is no interest at all, it is best not to proceed at the present time. But we should not close the door on a possible future following. However, if there is any interest at all, we should continue. We can be interested in a great variety of ways. We may be only curious, or we may be conditionally interested and wondering if our conditions will be met, or we may be fascinated and eager. All these shades of interest and any other variations are fine. One way to test out our interest is to see if this instruction appeals to us and we do it.

Find the two stories in the Gospel of Luke that we studied and meditated on, read them carefully, and continue the study and meditation. Even more, we might want to type or write them out, reformatting them — changing punctuation, starting a new paragraph every time another character speaks, etc. — so they read easily and communicate their meaning more effectively to us. And, as long as we have them out of the Bible and on pieces of paper, we might want to fold the papers and put them in pocket, briefcase, purse, or any-where they would be readily available. We never know when we might want to read these stories slowly, allowing them to shape our consciousness.

When we read them, a social situation we are part of may come to mind. Do not dismiss it as a distraction. Welcome it and look at it in the light of the passage. Sow the ideas from the passage into the situation. Do we see something we did not see before? However, do not decide on specific actions. In prayer-time we can decide to take an action in the light of what we see. But we should not commit to concrete ways of proceeding. That type of analysis and strategy is best done in day-time and in consultation with others.

Chapter Three ———————————————

Another Way of Praying

I F YOU ARE INTERESTED in following Jesus and learning the God–Self–Neighbor spiritual process as he presents it, pray the Lord's Prayer. This injunction makes sense because the embedded consciousness of the Lord's Prayer is the God–Self–Neighbor spiritual process. The ones praying begin by recognizing their communal being ("Our") and aligning themselves with the desires of God, making his name, kingdom, and will their driving passion. This passion keeps alive their everyday spiritual life the way bread keeps alive their everyday physical life. Then the ones praying ride this passion into the world of the neighbor, staking everything on the ability to forgive, to refuse to succumb to the temptation of destructive forces, and to refrain from actively doing evil. The structure of the Lord's Prayer is a succinct summary of the proper flow among God, Self, and Neighbor.

When we pray the Lord's Prayer, we participate in its consciousness and make it our own. The Lord's Prayer becomes our prayer. In theory, it is that simple. Yet when we try to do it, we bump into obstacles that we could not see in advance. They lurk in the conditioned mind, which has established ways of thinking and acting that make this prayer difficult to say correctly. We will have to work with these mental habits, evaluating and modifying them in order for the "consciousness transfer" to occur. As we do this, we will begin to know and do another way of praying.

Repetition, Devotion, Attention

When we pray the Lord's Prayer, we are praying someone else's prayer. We are not its author; and when we actually say it, we should not feel free to change the words. Most Christians have committed it to memory. They learned it relatively early in order to participate in community worship. So their history with it dates back to childhood, when mechanical memory was especially strong. Although we value mechanical memory, it has a downside when dealing with spiritual development.

Recently I was at a wedding reception where the minister was asked to say Grace Before Meals. He began abruptly. "A man was being chased by a lion and came to a cliff. He had no way to escape and looked back to see the lion approaching. Having run out of human options, he decided to pray. He knelt on the ground, closed his eyes, and prayed with all his heart. After a while he opened his eyes. The lion was fifteen feet away from the man. Much to his surprise, the lion was also kneeling and had his paws piously folded in prayer. The man strained to hear what the lion was saying. The words were familiar, especially to those assembled here tonight. The lion was saying. . . . "

At this point the minister gestured for us to join in. Everyone prayed with gusto and without missing a beat. "Bless us, O Lord, and these your gifts which we are about to receive from your bounty through Christ our Lord." With little or no difficulty, the group was able to draw this traditional prayer out of the bank of memory.

Although Grace Before Meals should not be compared to the Lord's Prayer, on one level they both belong to the same category. They are inherited prayers we have learned; and, in general, there are three ways to pray inherited prayers. "Repetition" says the prayer from memory, often in a collective context, and usually quite quickly. The words are mouthed, but no consistent attempt is made to tie the distracted mind to the meaning of the prayer as a whole or to each particular word or phrase. If we find ourselves praying the Lord's Prayer with this mindless inner state, we should stop. In the spiritual life habit is a powerful force for both development and lack of development. When it decreases awareness during prayer-time, it is a habit that should be broken.

"Devotion" says the prayer thoughtfully and concentrates on the transcendent source of all creation. God is being addressed and the mind struggles to adapt accordingly. However, the focus on God is vague and general. Often, the overriding attitude that permeates the prayer is worship. God is almighty, all-knowing, etc. We are limited in every respect. Therefore, whenever we pray we are always acknowledging a reality greater than ourselves. That is why we kneel and bow our heads during prayer. "Devotion" knows this truth and never lets it go. If we find ourselves praying the Lord's Prayer with devotion, we should continue as long as we know that there is a more developed way to proceed, and we walk that way from time to time. If we stay on the level of devotion, we will pray well in the community of believers. But there will be no transformation of consciousness, no spiritual development.

In the spiritual life habit is a powerful force for both development and lack of development. When it decreases awareness during prayer-time, it is a habit that should be broken.

"Attention" says the prayer thoughtfully and concretely, savoring each phrase, allowing it to open the mind to God. It tries to adapt the consciousness of the one praying to the embedded consciousness of the prayer, the God–Self–Neighbor spiritual process. In classical language, a concerted effort is made to put on the mind of Christ whose prayer it is. Naturally, this means saying the prayer more slowly than is possible in community services. But it also means we will have to study the prayer as a prerequisite for praying it. If we spend time with the meaning of each phrase, then when we pray those phrases, the meanings will return accompanied by appropriate affective states. Greater understanding facilitates greater awareness in the act of prayer.

Not from Earth to Heaven, from Heaven to Earth

We have memorized the Lord's Prayer, and we must deal with this fact if we are to use it as a practice for following Jesus. But the Lord's Prayer is often set within conventional prayer patterns. When we pray it in the context of those patterns, its distinctiveness may be compromised. It becomes a prayer for all seasons. When we are happy or when we are sad, when we eagerly wait for a child to be born or silently stay as an elder dies, when we hear of a plane going down or attend a church going up, when we stroll alone in the woods or gather together in Christian assembly, when we are filled with gratitude or emptied by grief, when we are driven to praise or dragged to repent, we reach for the Our Prayer. It is a prayer we know. The familiar and comforting words are on our lips.

Conventional prayer consciousness begins with a self-enclosed sense of who we are. We are earthlings, enlivened by positive experiences and threatened by negative experiences. When we enjoy positive experiences, our religious instincts kick in and we praise and thank the Source of All There Is. "Somebody Up There" likes us. When we suffer nega-tive experiences, we petition God in different ways. When we suffer because of our limitations, we pray to God, who is greater than we are and can do all things, to help us. When we suffer because of the sins of others, we pray to God for justice, to straighten out earthly affairs with divine judgment. When we recognize our own sinfulness has brought irreparable damage, we ask forgiveness, not only from those we have harmed but also from God, who sees all things. Depending on the circumstances, we relate to the transcendent God in different ways.

There is a dimension of us that lives in heaven where God, Self, and Neighbor are already in communion.

However, there is a common assumption behind these many expressions — gratitude, praise, help, forgiveness, etc. We are separate beings caught in the trammels of earth and trying to contact a superior being in heaven. Prayer is how we make this contact, and petitioning is never far from our mind. We want something and we can become desperate about getting it. There is a phrase that says it all: "We storm heaven with our prayers."

In the Gospel of Matthew Jesus introduces his prayer with a warning that it does not work like conventional prayers. "When you are praying, do not heap up empty phrases as the Gentiles do; for they think they will be heard because of their many words ... for your Father knows what you need before you ask" (Matt. 6:7–8). Beginning with human need, no matter what need it is, and then petitioning God at length to meet it is not the way the prayer of Jesus works.

His prayer is grounded in an opposite assumption. We do not begin as a solitary individual. We begin as "our," belonging to a common humanity and the earth. Even if we pray the Lord's Prayer in the silence of our heart, we are not alone because we recognize interrelationship as essential to who we are. Also, this "our" is aware of the God-grounding of our common humanity and earth; and this is the main concern of the prayer. Therefore, to pray the Lord's Prayer we must take a moment to adjust our consciousness to the first two words. When we do, we realize we do not begin on earth and petition heaven. We begin in heaven and bring heaven to earth. There is a dimension of us that lives in heaven where God, Self, and Neighbor are already in communion. We must enter this higher home and pray from that psychological and spiritual space.

This difference is crucial to the following of Jesus. In his study of Meister Eckhart, Cyprian Smith elaborates on it:

It is possible for human beings, living, thinking, and acting in God, to think, see, and do, as God does. Instead of standing within the created world, looking in it for signs of a God who is outside it, we stand within God, and it is the world which now appears outside. When we stand within the world, God appears as totally transcendent and "other." When we stand within God, however, it is the world which appears as "other," but not by any means transcendent; on the contrary, we are greater than it. It appears as a pale and imperfect reflection of the dazzling and brilliant Truth in which we are living and making our home.[6]

To most of us, this seems a staggering reversal. It may leave us confused about how this experience feels and how we could authentically say this is how we pray. It calls for more understanding and practice.

Heaven Is Within, Earth Is Without

More understanding is available in the Gospel of John. The storyteller shows us how Jesus moves from heaven to earth (John 13:3–5). "Jesus, knowing that the Father had given all things into his hands, and he had come from God and was going to God. . . . " This is equivalent to the opening intention of the Lord's Prayer: "Our Father, who are in heaven, hallowed be your name, your kingdom come, your will be done, on earth as it is heaven." Heaven is an image for a higher consciousness. When we are aware that our origin and destiny is God and, right here and now, the generative love of God who is called Father has given everything into our hands, we are "in heaven." Heaven is within.

This heavenly consciousness naturally flows into earthly action. That is because the nature of God is to give Spirit into creation, to manifest divine love in physical and social reality. "[Jesus] got up from the table, took off his outer robe, and tied a towel around himself. Then he poured water into a basin and began to wash the disciples' feet and wipe them with the towel that was tied around him" (John 3:4–5). The within is moving without. The God to whom the Self is connected is now moving the Self to connect with the Neighbor. The process is flowing, like water that pours from a poised pitcher into a waiting basin below.

Once again, this is a significant shift. Although we are using the cosmic imagery of heaven and earth, we are referring to a psychological and spiritual process. Walter Wink elaborates on it.

> Popular culture has tended to regard heaven (if it has regard for it at all) as a transcendent, otherworldly sphere qualitatively distinct from human life, to which the dead go if they have been good. What if we were instead to conceive of it as the realm of "withinness," the metaphorical "place" in which the spirituality of everything is "located," as it were. . . . Such a view of heaven finds it to be "nearer than breathing, closer than hand or foot," yet still transcendent. But its transcendence is not a transcendence of matter; . . . it is the transcendence of the "worldly" way of viewing reality, of the alienated order of existence, of egocentric ways of living, of idolatry of the part in defiance of the Whole, of the unrealized present by the consummation to come. It is transcendent by virtue of inwardness, invisibility, and futurity, not by remoteness and distance.[7]

The human person lives on the border of heaven and earth. When we are interiorly conscious of our relationship to God and neighbor, we are in heaven. When we allow that relationship to influence our lives, we are bringing heaven to earth.

Playing around with cosmic images like heaven and earth can be fun, but it can also be disconcerting. Later in this book I will suggest that hacking metaphors like "heaven and earth" is essential to cracking open the revelation of the Gospels and following Jesus. But a piece of my personal history reminds me of the difficulties.

We have a habit of reciting the Lord's Prayer without full intentionality. Sometimes we are at our worst, and it is mere repetition. Other times we are better, and it is done with devotion. But neither of these will turn prayer into spiritual development.

In the early sixties a Russian cosmonaut soared into outer space for the first time. When he returned to earth, he announced he had been to the home of God and no one was home. Heaven was empty, just endless space. My grandfather asked me what I thought of this remark. I mumbled something about not taking the symbol of heaven literally. From the look on my grandfather's face I knew he did not appreciate my evasiveness. He looked at me and said, "The son of a bitch didn't fly high enough."

There is always a tendency to take imagery about God literally. Heaven means heaven. Let's not play around. Even when we are aware that the language does not work that way, we find ourselves looking up when we pray or gesturing to the sky when we mention God. Images, especially images from childhood when the literal imagination was dominant, are deeply ingrained. Refuting it intellectually does not mean it is uprooted psychologically. It is difficult to heed the wise advice to take symbolic language seriously but not literally. But, if we are to follow Jesus into the God–Self–Neighbor spiritual process, it is necessary.

Where We Are

We took a basic outline of the God–Self–Neighbor spiritual process from two Gospel stories. But we want to deepen our grasp of that process until it becomes a steady feature of our consciousness. The recommended way to do this is to pray the Lord's Prayer, whose basic structure is the dynamic relationship among God, Self, and Neighbor. However, the Lord's Prayer must be prayed on its own terms. In order to do that, we have to work with some of our prayer habits.

We have a habit of reciting the Lord's Prayer without full intentionality. Sometimes we are at our worst, and it is mere repetition. Other times we are better, and it is done with devotion. But neither of these will turn prayer into spiritual development. We must do it mindfully if it is to be a practice that can open the mind to the flow of Spirit. Also, we carry the prayer project of conventional religiosity. It is the background of every act of prayer. Each prayer is pulled into its sphere of influence and reshaped according to what it is convinced is certain: we are separate creatures seeking the support of heaven. There is no other way to play it.

But Jesus has another way to play it. We are sons and daughters of God on a mission to bring heaven to earth. Heaven is the inner consciousness of our communion with God and Neighbor and earth is the uncharted territory where that spiritual truth has be lived out. In order to understand this movement more fully, It might be helpful to experience a prayer from another tradition that also has a "heaven to earth" and a "within to without" structure.

> May all beings be filled with joy and peace.
> May all beings everywhere,
> The strong and the weak,
> The great and the small,
> The mean and the powerful,
> The short and the long,
> The subtle and the gross.
>
> May all beings everywhere,
> Seen and unseen,

Dwelling far off or nearby,
Being or waiting to become:
May all beings be filled with lasting joy.

Let no one deceive another,
Let no one anywhere despise another,
Let no one out of anger or resentment
Wish suffering on anyone at all.

Just as a mother with her own life
Protects her child, her only child, from harm,
So within yourself let grow
A boundless love for all creatures.

Let your love flow outward through the universe,
To its height, its depth, its broad extent,
A limitless love, without hatred or enmity.

Then as you stand or walk,
Sit or lie down,
As long as you are awake,
Your life will bring heaven to earth.

> (Sutta Nipata, *Buddha's Discourse*
> *on Good Will*)

This prayer says it straightforwardly, "As long as you are awake, your life will bring heaven to earth."

Praying the Lord's Prayer keeps us awake. But before we say it, no matter where it might be — church, a wake, our own private moments — we should take time to reorient ourselves, pull consciousness inside and realize our already existing communion with God and Neighbor. In particular, we should situate ourselves within our God-groundedness and then open ourselves to the words and say them as the overflow of an already existing truth. At this stage we may not know what each of the phrases of the prayer means, but we can sense the overall dynamic and allow it to carry us along.

Say it in this intentional way twice a day. Don't immediately evaluate whether you are doing it right. Just do it. After a week, notice how you feel when you say the prayer this way. Describe how you feel to yourself.

Chapter Four

Reclaiming Religious Passion

RECENTLY I WAS HAVING BREAKFAST with a high school classmate. He looked up from his waffle at my 240-pound frame and said, "I was reading something you wrote. Are you really that religious?"

The tone of his voice was incredulous. All the inflection was on the word, "really." His expectation was, as my father would say, "Say it ain't so, Joe." But I suspected what he meant by religious and what I meant by religious were two different things. It was one of those questions that should be explored before it is answered. But this was not the place or the time to get into a complex conversation. Besides, my eggs were getting cold.

I said, "Yeah."

"That's okay," he assured me. "There's nothing wrong with it."

I wasn't comforted. He tolerated my religious bent, considering it harmless, a personal idiosyncrasy. But I did not think about it that way. I saw it as a raw instinct that I did not choose but had to live with. It was thrust upon me, just there. In my view, religious passion comes with the territory of the human. It will not be denied, but it can be misplaced. The result is what religious traditions call idolatry, conferring ultimacy on some nonultimate object or person. Therefore, it is essential to get it right, to tie ourselves (that is what the word "religion" means) to what is truly ultimate. It is religious passion that drives me to follow Jesus. For what I hear Jesus saying on every page of the Gospels is: "I know how to fulfill that passion in a way beyond what you can imagine." Can we resist that enticement?

We are not apologists arguing with unbelievers. We are secularly influenced followers of Jesus reconvincing ourselves.

Previous cultures assumed people were aware of and respected their intrinsic relationship to ultimate reality. It was taken for granted. But in a secular culture, which restricts awareness to the physical, social, and mental dimensions, this is not the case. Therefore, we have to explicitly look at this area of experience, articulate its dynamics, and recover its significance. At first, this may seem like an inconvenience, but actually it is an advantage. Dialoguing with the secular cultural mood allows us to examine and strengthen one of the driving forces of following Jesus. Also, this cultural mood is not just "out there." As they say in popular parlance, "Everyone drinks from the Kool-Aid." The cultural mood is a pervasive atmosphere that subtly shapes our consciousness. We are not apologists arguing with unbelievers. We are secularly influenced followers of Jesus reconvincing ourselves.

Spiritual but Not Religious

Lately, secular consciousness has been flirting with transcendence. It is captured in a phrase that has a decent amount of currency: "I'm spiritual but not religious." This means the ones speaking admit to spiritual sensibilities. Their consciousness is not confined to the physical, social, and mental dimensions. They are aware of a spiritual dimension that Lao Tzu characterized as "lingering like gossamer, barely hinting at existence; but when you draw upon it, it is inexhaustible." But, at the same time, they do not belong to any faith community or religious organization. Their spiritual sensibility is native and natural, not dependent on a religious tradition. Previously, the religious and the spiritual were identified with one another. Now they can be distinguished, opening a respectable middle position between secularity and religion.

If we leave it at that, it is a legitimate distinction. The spiritual comes with the territory of creation. It is present and active prior to the emergence in history of religious forms that express and communicate it. So, in principle, the two can be distinguished, and the spiritual can be appreciated without the benefit of a religious tradition. But, in practice, the religious and the spiritual are usually connected. The default human consciousness concentrates largely on the physical and social dimensions. Moving into an awareness of the spiritual and consistently inhabiting that consciousness takes guidance and support. The presence of a community and tradition is usually needed if the spiritual dimension is to be taken seriously. The spiritual and the religious can be distinguished, but the distinction should not develop into a separation.

However, there is another implication of this distinction that has to be considered, one that is very closely connected to following Jesus. When the spiritual and religious are separated, the spiritual is often described in terms of human transcendence. We cannot be reduced to our physical, social, and mental dimensions. We are a little bit more than our bodies, social relationships, and mental conditioning. This transcendence gives us a sense we are more than reactors to events. We can never be completely defined by circumstances. We are always capable of going against the grain, of formulating responses that push against what is going on. In traditional language, this awareness of ourselves as transcendent might be called the discovery of "soul."

Study the Fence

This is fine as far as it goes, but it does not go far enough. The spiritual sensibility of human transcendence has to be complemented by the religious awareness of a transcendent source. The discovery of soul is the first step in the religious process of awakening to God. This process should not be short-circuited.

One of the tried and true paths to religious awareness is reflecting on the obvious fact of our finitude. On our birthdays we celebrate our coming into this world. But the flip side of this entry is that the world had been going on for a long time without us. There was a "before us." This thought about the past might project us into a thought about the future — there will be a time when we will not be here. We will die and the world will go on. There will be an "after us." When we become aware of this radical finitude, we might experience pain and be tempted to look away. Our ego does not want us to take into account this basic condition of being human. It urges us to get on with life with little or no knowledge of what life itself is all about.

This ability to bracket ultimate questions is a valued feature of secular consciousness. People can live rich and meaningful lives without ever considering whether life itself is meaningful. John Haught, a theologian, holds the position that without cosmic meaning individual meaning is threatened. Will Provine of Cornell University begs to differ.

> My own life is filled with meaning. I am married to a talented and beautiful woman, have two great sons, live on a beautiful farm with lots of old but good farm machinery, teach at a fine university where the students are excellent, and have many wonderful friends. But I will die and be forgotten.... Haught will have a tough time

convincing me that my life is meaningless just because there is no cosmic meaning for it.[8]

If we work it right, we can enjoy individual and social meaning. Why go further? Looking for cosmic meaning is precarious and open to debate. Looking for religious meaning is just not needed.

There is a wonderful Hindu depiction of this restriction of consciousness. Dr. Rachel Remen uses it to great effect in her book *Kitchen Table Wisdom*.[9] Joseph Campbell is conducting a workshop for doctors, showing and commenting on sacred images from world religions. One of them shows the god Shiva dancing in a ring of bronze flames. His many arms hold symbols of abundant spiritual life. One foot is up in the air and one foot is positioned on the back of a little man who is bent over, totally absorbed in studying a leaf. The doctors were taken with the little man and asked Campbell about him. Laughing, Campbell told them the little man was so engrossed in the material world that he did not even know the living God was dancing on his back. In our culture, to varying degrees, we are all that little man.

But religious traditions urge us to stir from this sleep. They encourage us to follow the clues in our sense of radical contingency. Anthony De Mello told a story about a young lion awakening in captivity. As he explored his environment, he came upon groups of lions debating politics, teaching the young, caring for the sick, writing and acting out dramas, etc. Each group invited him to join them and told him of the importance of their work. Then the young lion noticed an old, craggy lion off by himself. He approached him and confided that he did not know what to do with his life. The old lion gave only one line of advice, "Study the fence." The fundamental indisputable fact that should be seriously pondered is that we are fenced in by birth and death.

What will serious pondering of our finitude lead to?

The Mystery of Spirit

It will move us into a sense of an immanent-transcendent reality that is the permeating context of life, a reality that is more than temporal passage but is intimately related to ongoing events. Finite life senses infinite life; contingent life senses absolute life. It is this sense of a More, a Whole, an Encompassing, an Ultimate that is the necessary psychological grounding to grasp the God–Self–Neighbor process. An increasingly preferred word for this sense of Ultimacy is Mystery. "Mystery" satisfies the contemporary taste for "leanness." It says something, but it does not say too much. More importantly, it does not claim the Mystery will be solved in the way a problem is solved. The Mystery remains mysterious even after a revelation. In fact, it becomes more mysterious after a revelation. Therefore, there is always an element of not-knowing at the core of knowing. In metaphorical language, our sense of the immanent-transcendent Mystery is always a matter of light and darkness.

A second preferred word for this immanent-transcendent reality is Spirit. "Spirit" cannot be construed as one object or subject among others. It is a reality that energizes and elevates particular objects and subjects without being confined to them. Spirit can go into another reality without displacing any of that reality. It is something all discrete beings share according to their capacity to receive it and express it. If "Mystery" conveys the sense of transcendence (how this reality is always more), "Spirit" conveys the sense of immanence (how this reality is present in everyone and everything). When this religious sensibility is a firmly established form of perception, people intuit that their communion with this immanent-transcendent reality called the Mystery of Spirit is the mission of human life. In more traditional language, it is the path of salvation.

Becoming aware of this Mystery of Spirit at the center of our own being and then, surprisingly, realizing it is at the center of every being can be quite a trip. It is the blessedness that Jesus praised. "Blessed are the pure of heart for they shall see God" (Matt. 5:8). The purity of our own heart consists in understanding we are dependent on the Mystery of Spirit and permeated by its energies. Knowing this in ourselves, we see it in others and in everything. We work from the inside out. The Mystery of Spirit may sustain and transform all there is, but we cannot discern it unless we first know its love is sustaining and transforming us. Charity begins at home.

When we become aware and convinced of the Mystery of Spirit, a new desire begins to rise in us. We want to be united to this Mystery and live out of it. We are becoming passionately religious, realizing how important it is to tie ourselves to what is truly Ultimate. If we are disturbed by this sudden surge of passion, I have some advice to pass on to us that was given to me. "That's okay. There's nothing wrong with it."

Where We Are

We have taken a journey of consciousness, traveling the secular path from the certainty of the physical, social, and mental dimensions to the subtlety of human spiritual transcendence and then to the grounding of human transcendence in the Mystery of Spirit. This journey has taken us beneath God-talk to uncover the primordial situation that makes it legitimate. In the process, we have adjusted our imagination to correct a common mistaken assumption. When we are told to unite with God, it is not an injunction to find a Superior Being and make a connection. It entails waking up to the Mystery of Spirit that pulses through and transcends everything, especially ourselves. Hopefully, this journey has helped us to reclaim our religious passion, the desire to commune with and serve what is Ultimate. If it has not, we must find another path. Without religious passion, the major reason for persevering in the following of Jesus disappears.

This conversion of consciousness about God complements the conversion of consciousness about prayer. Both John the Baptist and Jesus said conversion was necessary in order to enter into the Kingdom of God (Matt. 3:2; 4:17). The Greek word for conversion is *metanoia*. It means "change your mind" or "go beyond your present way of thinking." How exactly the mind has to change may differ from one culture to another. But the following of Jesus always entails communing with God in prayer, so today we have to clear both a religious path and a cultural path, removing any thinking about prayer and God that will not allow us to hear Jesus.

Hearing Jesus and the Gospels means listening to the words and receiving the communication. However, these words are not precise and technical language. They are poetic and ecstatic utterings. Even in their written state, we can sense their original rocketing voice. They do not desire to communicate ideas. They hope to sweep us up into the reality that is manifesting itself through them. That is high ambition, and to achieve it we must actively cooperate. If we want to deeply receive Jesus' revelation about the God–Self–Neighbor spiritual process, we must learn to hack metaphor.

Chapter Five ────────────────────────────────

Hacking Metaphor

R OBINSON DAVIES, a Canadian novelist, once remarked, "An atheist is someone who can't hack metaphor." I don't know about atheists. But to use the Gospels to know and do the God–Self–Neighbor spiritual process, it is imperative to hack metaphor.

The Sacramental Imagination

In the last chapter, we explored the sense of an immanent-transcendent reality; and, recognizing the cultural reluctance to say too much, we called it the Mystery of Spirit. This naming establishes some important negative ground rules: never think the human mind can exhaustively know Mystery, and never think spirit is one object or subject among many. But, however important this initial description is, it is only a skeletal identification. And the Gospels as a whole, and Jesus in particular, are never satisfied with bare bones.

Jesus experienced the Mystery of Spirit in a certain way and he tried to express and communicate that experience to his disciples so they could have a similar experience. His way of expression and communication was intimately connected to

how he experienced it. Yet a general law of human consciousness remained operative. The physical and social dimensions
are more available to consciousness than the spiritual. When
the spiritual manifests itself in and through the physical and
social, it is natural to talk about it in terms of physical and
social dynamics. This is often called the sacramental imagination: for those who have eyes to see all of creation reveals
the Mystery of Spirit (Matt. 13:16). Jesus has these eyes.

Jesus' actions open up the Mystery of Spirit. He may be
breaking bread, or making mud, or placing his hands on children, or sticking his fingers in ears, or walking on a wave, or
taking off his outer garments, or crying outside a tomb, or
sleeping in a boat, or touching a leper, or pouring water in a
basin, or offering a dipped morsel, or throwing himself on the
ground, or going up a mountain, or going off by himself, or
sitting wearied by a well, or raising his eyes, or overturning
tables, or withering a fig tree, or unwithering an arm, or getting out of a boat, or freeing the animals from the temple, or
walking toward Jerusalem, or riding on a donkey, or shouting outside the tomb of one he loves, or — whatever it is, it
is more than arbitrary. It is a revelation of the Mystery of
Spirit, telling us something about what God is like and how
we should relate to divine reality.

Jesus' words work the same way as his actions. He may be
speaking body words about counting the hairs of the head,
or washing each other's feet, or grinding teeth, or having eyes
that do not see and ears that do not hear, or lips that are not
in sync with the heart, or a heart that is hard, or a forgiving

heart, or a heart from which good or evil flows, or a mouth that food enters on its way to the stomach, or a foot that tramples savorless salt, or a body that is bent over, or a heart that is meek and humble, or — but it is always somehow about the Mystery of Spirit.

Or Jesus may mention the animal world of birds nesting, or foxes having holes, or snakes and scorpions being stepped on, or fish and eggs rather than snakes and scorpions being handed to children, or pigs feeding on pearls, or sheep listening for their names, or a mother hen gathering her chicks, or dogs scrounging scraps, or vultures gathering, or a fatted calf whose number is up, or a camel squeezing through the eye of a needle, or a gnat swimming in a wine cup, or sparrows falling, or moths munching, or birds not needing barns, or wolves crossdressing, or snakes brooding, or worms dying not, or — but it is always somehow about the Mystery of Spirit.

Or Jesus' speech may include the universe with talk of good earth, or wasted soil, or trees bearing fruit, or a sky with written names, or thorns without figs, or wheat and weeds together, or the sun losing its light, or the moon bleeding, or water springing up from within, or lilies flourishing and perishing, or the earth quaking, or the sea heaving, or a reed shaking, or the weather signals of the sky, or the fate of seeds on different soils, or — but it is always somehow about the Mystery of Spirit.

Or Jesus may comment on human enterprises — on physicians healing themselves, or on farmers sowing, or on merchants haggling, or on fathers running, or on women sweeping, or on shepherds searching, or on sons disobeying, or on workers grumbling, or on servants drinking, or on masters returning, or on debtors begging, or on priests posturing, or on lawyers nitpicking, or on judges stonewalling, or on widows persisting, or on fishermen casting, or on tenants scheming, or on leaders plotting, or on guests excusing, or on builders quitting, or on kings retreating, or on children coming, or on the rich walking away, or on women crying, or on his disciples scattering, or on — but it is always somehow about the Mystery of Spirit.

On one level the deeds and words of Jesus are about the physical and social dimensions as they were observed and understood in his culture. On another level, they are about the Mystery of Spirit. If we are to learn to do the God–Self–Neighbor spiritual process as Jesus taught it, we must first learn how to move from the level of the physical and the social to the level of the Mystery of Spirit. We must become adept at hacking metaphor.

Getting It and Getting It Right

Most of the characters in the Gospels stumble over Jesus' metaphors at one time or another. They either are totally oblivious the words are meant metaphorically, or they cannot make the correct connection from the physical and social realms to the spiritual. The most celebrated stumbler is Nicodemus (John 3:1–10). Jesus confides to him, "Very truly,

I tell you, no one can see the Kingdom of God without being born from above." Nicodemus responds, "How can anyone be born after growing old? Can one enter a second time into the mother's womb to be born?" There has been a serious lack of communication. What Jesus is saying and what Nicodemus is hearing are two different things. The problem lies in the metaphor.

> *Most of the characters in the Gospels stumble over Jesus' metaphors at one time or another.*

Jesus is using a physical image of birth to point to a spiritual process, but Nicodemus cannot follow this move. He is stuck on birth as a physical event. That makes Jesus' speech nonsensical. The picture of a grown man entering a second time into his mother's womb is ludicrous. The conversation has seriously ground to a halt. Jesus attempts to restart it by piling on another metaphor. "The wind blows were it chooses, and you hear the sound of it, but you do not know where it comes from or where it goes. So is everyone who is born of the Spirit." This is not much help to the flat-footed Nicodemus. "How can these things be?" He is befuddled.

But we should not be too hard on Nicodemus. What is it about birth that reveals the Mystery of Spirit? Later in the Gospel, Jesus will tell his disciples, "When a woman is in labor, she has pain because her hour has come. But when a child is born, she no longer remembers the anguish because of the joy of having brought a human being into the world" (John 16:21). That line of thought is pertinent to the experience of losing Jesus in death and finding him in a new and risen form. But it does not seem to fit the conversation between Jesus and Nicodemus. Both we and Nicodemus will have to try another connection. And what is it about free-wheeling, noisy wind whose origin and destination we do not know? What is the truth about the Mystery of Spirit that the wind is expressing and trying to communicate to us? It is not easy to be a dialogue partner with Jesus.

Another aspect of hacking metaphors is knowing when to quit. Not every aspect of the metaphoric situation fits the relationship to Spirit. Often when we find a connection that illumines our minds or inspires our will, we plod on, thinking there must be more gold in them there hills. But the better advice may be to drop that metaphor and find another. Someone compared metaphors to eating a fig. The idea is to suck out the pulp and juice and discard the skin. This is a healthy attitude because it prevents images from becoming "stock" and losing their metaphoric invention. Suddenly they are no longer metaphors but literal truths. This causes a great deal of confusion, especially with the Gospel images of "Father" and "King."

Sometimes stories are crafted that take up metaphors and expand them. When this happens, the story provides clues for how the metaphor might reveal our relationship to Spirit. For example, the naked metaphor of "Father" is fleshed out by the words and deeds of the father in the story of the Prodigal Son. This giving, welcoming, and reconciling father helps us hack the metaphor. Still, there has to be a considerable amount of cooperation between the speech of Jesus and the mind of whomever hears or reads his words. At one point Jesus' disciples tell him, "Finally, you are speaking plainly" (John 16:29). This sounds like relief that Jesus has moved away from metaphors into more direct description and analysis. But there is a very good reason for staying in the world of metaphor.

Metaphors set the conditions for personal discovery. When the listeners get the connection correctly, they receive it as a revelation. It is not just second-hand information. "So that's how Jesus sees it." Neither is it speculative knowledge. "That's very interesting." It is the type of knowing that rings true, that resonates both cognitively and affectively. As they hack the metaphors, they are grasped and held by their truth. This personal realization establishes the insight as a structure of perception. It is not a fleeting thought that will be ousted by the conventional categories that occupy most of our mental space. It enters into serious competition with other categories. The word has been heard and the thorns do not choke it (Luke 8:7).

Hacking metaphors is playful, but it is not easy work. It demands knowledge of the metaphoric area and also some inchoate and intuitive sense of the Mystery of Spirit. When they come together, revelation occurs. Some think when we get it right, the revelation is self-authenticating. The revelation carries with it the unshakeable sense that it is right. I have never been privileged to have that type of confirmation. But I do know that when the revelation carries a sense of abundant life, obedience to it seems to be exquisitely appropriate. However, it does not eliminate the precariousness in the project of hacking metaphors.

Where We Are

We started by reflecting on my morning meditation on Jesus stories to get a sense of what following him entails. It requires entering into the God–Self–Neighbor spiritual process that Jesus tried to teach to his disciples and to others and by which he himself lived. The dynamics of this process are seen in Jesus' skilled teaching of the lawyer by using the parable of the Good Samaritan and his own prayer and conflict struggle in Gethsemane. As contemporary followers, we need to reframe how we pray and reclaim our religious passion in order to know and do the God–Self–Neighbor process. But this process can only go forward as a following of Jesus if we learn to hack the metaphors that express and communicate the Mystery of Spirit that flows so abundantly through him. The first metaphor to hack is the image for the Self, the reality of who we are that is the medium of communion with God and the Neighbor. We are heart.

Chapter Six _____

Self: Identifying with the Heart

A FTER THE CRUCIFIXION of Jesus, two of his followers
are escaping Jerusalem for Emmaus when the risen Lord
suddenly walks along with them[10] (Luke 24:13–35). "Their
eyes are kept from recognizing him." This was not because
Jesus' physical appearance was disguised or transformed. It
was because they did not understand who he really was and
so, in this sense, they had never fully or correctly recognized
him, even in his pre-crucifixion days. In a wonderful irony,
they show this lack of understanding by telling Jesus about
himself. In their minds, he was a much-loved prophet who
was a victim of the religious authorities and whose execution
undercut their hopes. They even know the women's report of
an empty tomb, a vision of angels, and an investigation of the
empty tomb by some of their company. None of this resulted
in seeing Jesus.

When Jesus hears this reductionist rendition of his identity and mission, he calls these fellow travelers foolish and
slow of heart. "Foolish and slow of heart" combine to name
their problem. They are foolish because they tell Jesus' life
without reference to God, and only fools say there is no God

(Ps. 14:1). This foolishness contributes to their slowness of heart. In Gospel spirituality, the heart is connected to the eyes. When the heart burns, fire pushes up the chest and flows out through the eyes. When the heart is not on fire, there can only be darkness. "The eye is the lamp of the body. So if your eye is healthy, it is because your whole body is full of light. But if your eye is unhealthy, it is because your whole body is full of darkness. If then the light in you is darkness, how great will the darkness be" (Matt. 6:22–23). The body full of light is the burning heart. To be slow of heart does not mean to be without heart. It means that these two deserting followers have not allowed their spiritual center to influence how they think about Jesus and how they act in relation to him. Therefore, they are in the dark about who Jesus is and what actually happened in Jerusalem. This is about to change.

Spiritual knowing happens when we open to the flow of life in the center of our being and it enters and elevates our minds and wills.

Jesus remedies their slowness of heart by opening up the scriptures that reveal the truth about him. Later when he does his paradigmatic Eucharistic gesture — taking bread, giving thanks, breaking, and giving — their eyes are opened and they recognize him. Jesus disappears, and the two followers tell one another the reason they were able to recognize him.

"Were not our hearts burning within us while he was talking to us on the road, while he was opening the scriptures to us?" They are able to perceive the risen Lord only when their hearts are on fire, only when they allow their spiritual center to elevate their minds and wills.

Previously, Jesus had done the same Eucharistic gesture and interpreted it. "This is my body given for you. Do this in memory of me" (Luke 22:19). But then his followers were face to face with him. They recognized him in the conventional way of the senses — the shape of his body and the sound of his voice. However, they did not grasp the import of what he was doing and saying. That is why they are so confused about his passion and death and have the whole story wrong. Now, when identification by the senses is not available, they are required to recognize him spiritually in his Eucharistic gesture. Strangely enough, the loss of his physical presence makes possible a perception of his spiritual presence and a better understanding of who he always was.

The Knowing Heart

The burning heart that provides light for the eyes is a physical metaphor for how the spiritual center flows into the mind and illuminates it so it can see the workings of Spirit in the world. The shorthand phrase for this process is "spiritual knowing" or "the knowing heart." The resulting illumination of the mind is different from dispassionate intellectual comprehension, although intellectual comprehension can be a first step toward spiritual knowing. Spiritual knowing does not take place in the upper reaches of the mind. It does not grasp and capture persons, objects, and events outside the knower. It knows by communion, by uniting us to what we perceive.

Spiritual knowing works like the physical heart. The heart is an organ, enclosed in a cage of ribs, that pumps blood throughout the body. After the pumped blood has circulated throughout the body, it returns to the heart to start the process all over again. Again and again, the heart gives life to the entire body. Our spiritual center operates analogously. This center pumps life into the whole mind-body organism, renewing it over and over again. In order for the mind and will to stay filled with life, they have to return to the spiritual center and then go out from it again. Therefore, our spiritual center is like yeast in dough that makes the whole mass rise and transforms it into bread. It is like carrying grain in the folds of our robe and suddenly the grain overflows. It is like catching so many fish our nets are bursting. It is like perfume whose fragrance fills the whole room. Spiritual knowing happens when we open to the flow of life in the center of our being and it enters and elevates our minds and wills.

Therefore, the spiritual center is like the heart; and when we hack the metaphor, we get a sense of how it functions, how it operates in the entire mind-body organism. But heart is only one metaphor. Our spiritual center has many names. It is called: Soul, Gate of Heaven and Earth, Pearl of Great Price, Treasure Hidden in a Field, Transcendent Self, Salt of the Earth, Rock, Light of the World, Spirit, the Sapphire at the Bottom of the Sea, Image of God, Child of God, the Virgin Point, Heaven on Earth, Closet, Hidden Room, etc. Each of these metaphors tells us different yet complementary truths about our spiritual center. So a spiritual exercise to help us "enter the heart" is to move from metaphor to metaphor until our minds adapt and make maps to this hidden territory.

The Self

The heart is the spiritual center; and the spiritual center is the Self in the God–Self–Neighbor process. This is our true and ultimate identity, incorporating all other subidentities into it. It is not something we can step back from for there is no space behind it to inhabit. It is not one component of our total make-up, something we could put on a list and say we have. It is us. Rainer Maria Rilke knew it.

> And if the earthly no longer knows your name
> whisper to the silent earth: I am flowing
> to the flashing water: I am.

We must learn to identify with this spiritual center. This entails disidentifying with other ways we imagine ourselves. We are used to identifying with our competitive edges, with the physical, psychological, and social benefits that separate us from others. I am in better health, have a higher I.Q., and have more money than someone else. But, alas, I am also in poorer health, have a lower I.Q., and have less money than another person. Within this way of thinking we alternate between being better or worse off; we swing back and forth between pitying those who have less and envying those who have more. Identity by comparison is a roller coaster ride.

In contrast, identifying with the Self situates us in a relational world of unity. On the one hand, the Self opens to God. In the theology of the Christian East, this is what "deep heart" means.

> "The heart is deep" (Ps. 64:7) ... means that the human person is a profound mystery, that I understand only a very small part of myself, that my conscious ego-awareness is far from exhausting the total reality of my authentic Self. But it signifies more than that. It implies that in the innermost depths of my heart I transcend the bounds of my created personhood and discover within myself the direct and unmediated presence of the living God. Entry into the deep heart means that I experience myself as God-sourced, God-enfolded, God-transfigured. Although sinful and unworthy, I am yet enabled to say with humble confidence, "His life is mine.... " Eventually by God's grace and mercy the seeker attains the "deep heart" which is the Divine spark within us, the innermost sanctuary where God the Trinity dwells, the point of encounter between time and eternity, between space and infinity, between the created and the Uncreated.[11]

On the other hand, the Self opens to neighbor. When Jesus sees the crowds, his heart goes out to them (Mark 8:2). We must forgive our brothers and sisters from our heart (Matt. 18:35). It is important not to lose heart in the struggle for social justice (Luke 10:27). The heart produces goodness toward others (Luke 6:45). When we have identified with our spiritual center, comparison is integrated into the deeper truth of communion with God and Neighbor.

Where We Are

Through hacking the metaphor of "heart," we have come to greater clarity about the God–Self–Neighbor spiritual process. Although the fullness of who we are includes physical bodies, social relationships, and mental processes, especially the formation and establishment of the ego, the Self in question is the knowing heart. This spiritual center is our ultimate identity. We live in relationship to the Mystery of Spirit from whom we receive Spirit and in relationship to our neighbor to whom we give Spirit. Therefore, the knowing heart has no existence independent of the flow from God and the flow to neighbor.

When the hearts of Jesus' two fellow travelers burned, they were able to see the spiritual dynamics at work in physical and social events of his life. Their slow hearts sped up. In particular, they were able to hack the metaphor of his Eucharistic gesture — taking, thanking, breaking, and giving. The taking and thanking signified that Jesus was receiving life at every moment from his loving Father, the self-giving transcendent Source of Life. The breaking and giving signified that he was offering the life he was receiving to others. This was what was going on throughout his entire life and this was what was going on in his passion and crucifixion. Only the burning heart knows this. We are our spiritual center, ever receiving life and ever giving it away.

What are the dynamics of receiving and thanking?

Chapter Seven

God: Receiving and Thanking

FOR A NUMBER of years I was lucky enough to live in an apartment that had a porch. On late summer nights I would sit there on a lawn chair with a nightcap handing myself over to the darkness. Occasionally, the moon and stars would provide dazzle.

One night a friend joined me. He was in a reflective mood and began reminiscing about all the people who had intersected his life "for the good." Some stories were about people who rode to the rescue with guns blazing. Other stories were about people who didn't even know they were helping, secret allies or, as we would say theologically, actual graces. I reciprocated, sharing a list of people who lived fondly in my memory. Gradually, we were in an atmosphere of gratitude, breathing it in and getting high.

I have often noticed that gratitude fills us up from within, sometimes so full we spill over in tears. It opens us to the world of lifegiving relationships and counters the temptation to think we are alone and separate. When the sense of isolation occupies our consciousness, we become sullen and downcast, cut off from lifegiving energies. We lose zest.

I asked my friend if he was ever grateful for life itself. Not for friends and companions, or for good things that had happened, but just for life itself, sheer, unadulterated existence. I had recently read a book that had called this form of thankfulness "ontological gratitude." I was checking it out.

My friend did not reply quickly. He thought and sipped his drink. "Mostly, I just take being alive for granted. But, when I get a bad health scare, and I've had a few, I thank God I'm alive." It was a validation of Paul Tillich's insight that the shock of nonbeing illumines being. Otherwise, being alive is the necessary backdrop for adventures, and adventures capture consciousness.

As often happens, this intellectual turn in the conversation killed it. The thrill of gratitude dissolved into other topics. As I look back, we were feeling around for something in the dark. We touched it, but still there was more beyond our reach.

The Self-Giving Spirit

The Mystery of Spirit is totally self-giving, pouring itself into creation. When it pours itself into human creation, Jesus calls it "Father in heaven, or "my Father," or "your Father," or simply "Father." This Father in heaven makes the sun rise on the evil and on the good, and sends rain on the righteous and the unrighteous (Matt. 5:45). Spirit is unconditional love, giving itself to all regardless of their moral status. When the Beloved Disciple, resting on the heart of Jesus, asks him who will betray him, Jesus says the one to whom he gives the morsel after he has dipped it (John 13:25). In other words, Jesus will give himself to one he knows will betray him. His self-giving is coming from the nature of the relationship between the Father and the Son rather than the perceived value of the recipient. Put anachronistically, Jesus knew full well Judas's intent but gave him communion anyway.

In the Gospels, Jesus thinks it is extremely important to know about this self-giving nature of God, the Mystery of Spirit. After he has taught his disciples to pray, he spends time assuring them that, in traditional language, their prayers are always answered because of the nature of the one to whom they pray (Luke 11:1–13). Humans often give reluctantly like a man who at midnight is in bed. A friend knocks on his door asking for bread. It seems a friend of the knocker has suddenly arrived and hospitality demands he offer him food. Unfortunately, he has none. The man in bed may tell his friend to go away because it is late and he has locked his door. But if the petitioner persists, the man in bed will get up and give him bread — if not out of friendship then out of the possibility of being shamed when the other people in the village hear about his refusal.

However, it is not like that with the Mystery of Spirit. It gives because that is what it does. It does not need to be badgered or shamed. So the disciples can ask, seek, and knock with confidence. What they ask for will be given, what they seek will be found, and what they knock on will be opened. If these encouragements are taken, they will open the hearts of the disciples, turning them from stone to flesh, from slow to fast, from fearful to receptive. They might even surmise that the real one who asks, seeks, and knocks is the Spirit who is asking, seeking, and knocking on the human heart. "Here I stand, knocking at the door; if you hear my voice and open the door, I will come into you..." (Rev. 3:20).

The heavenly Father only gives the Holy Spirit. We may ask for a little red wagon, but the Spirit will arrive. The Father is Spirit, and that is what God gives.

Then, Jesus takes another tack to convince them of the self-giving Spirit. If their children would ask them for a fish, they would not give them a snake; or if they would ask them for an egg, they would not hand them a scorpion. This time it is not a story about a reluctant giver, but about the eager givers that fathers themselves are when it comes to their children. Then Jesus says they do this even though they are evil. So how much more will the heavenly Father give the Holy Spirit to those who ask him? If human fathers who are evil are not deceptive, passing off snakes as fish and scorpions as eggs, then the heavenly Father, who is good, will certainly not be deceptive.

However, there is a twist. The heavenly Father only gives the Holy Spirit. We may ask for a little red wagon, but the Spirit will arrive. The Father is Spirit, and that is what God gives. To top it off, the Father does not give the Spirit out of obligation or with any ulterior motive, even the hope that the Spirit will equip us to be moral. It is a matter of pleasure. It is the Father's pleasure to give us the Kingdom (Luke 12:32). God likes to give Spirit.

These images and stories eventually contribute to the idea of grace as the essence of the Divine. God is a free unconditional flow of life into us. In the first moment, this flow of life constitutes us in existence. Existence is the first gift, and its gift character never goes away. This insight does not immediately square with how we usually think about our life. It seems giftedness might apply to the very beginning when, without any desire or effort on our part, we emerge out of the meeting of seed and egg. But once we are born, we seem to be on our own, breathing and eating in interdependence with the universe. Given the gift of life by God through the medium of our parents, we now have that life as a possession to be appreciated and cared for until it runs out. But this way of thinking might be too narrow. Spiritual traditions think the umbilical cord to God is never cut. When we understand this spiritual truth, gratitude will become a fountain within us springing up into everlasting life (John 4:14).

Children of God

The Gospel of John begins by assuring us that the Word, the outer expression of God, is truly God (John 1:1–18).

"The Word was with God and the Word was God." Although this seems definite, it would take Christian tradition nearly five hundred years to chisel this truth in stone. This identity-in-distinction between the Word and God was from the beginning. In other words, it is essential and there never was a time when it was not. "In the beginning" translates into always and everywhere. This Word is the medium of creation, bringing all things into being. This being is life. Therefore all things are sustained by God's life, but in people this life becomes a light. In other words, the Source of Life enters into human consciousness. We become aware of both God's life in us and what God's life allows us to understand about the world. This careful theological phrasing wants to make this point, a point that will ground the entire life, death, ascension, and resurrection of Jesus, the Word Made Flesh.

When the Word brings life that becomes light in us, we become the children of God. "He came unto his own, but his own received him not. But to all who received him, who believed in his name, he gave power to become children of God, who were born, not of blood or of the will of the flesh or of the will of man, but of God." Children of God are born in a specific way. They are not solely physical beings, totally branded by the blood that appears at the first moment of childbirth — natural generation. Nor are they merely the products of sexual attraction and the ensuing will of the flesh — human choice. Nor are they just part of the human social contracts where males desire children as economic capital — man's decision. They are generated by receiving Jesus, the Word. The Father gives himself to the Son, and the Son gives the Father and himself to us. Our task is to receive the self-giving Mystery of Spirit.

Rock

There is a quality about this relational flow of life that Jesus and the Gospels emphasize. It is not susceptible to destruction or loss. It is not like things on earth "where moth and rust consume and thieves break in and steal" (Matt. 6:19–21). Therefore, we should treasure this "heavenly" relationship. If we do, it will fill consciousness because "where our treasure is, there will be our heart." This relationship will become the center of who we are and spread out into mind, body, and world.

Jesus alludes to this indestructibility in one of his training sessions with his disciples (Luke 10:17–20). They have returned from a mission where they discovered they had power over demons. Jesus is delighted with this self-knowledge. He reaffirms their awareness by telling them that he saw Satan fall like lightning from the sky. They really do have power, not only over demons but also over the prince of demons. This is precisely what they should be doing and they should recognize they are following Jesus when they do it. "See, I have given you authority to tread on snakes and scorpions, and over all the power of the enemy; and nothing will hurt you."

It may be common sense to avoid snakes and scorpions, but Jesus does not recommend that. His power is to put them out of business. Although this is a truly dangerous activity, they will not be harmed. But how can this be? Jesus' treading on snakes and scorpions will bring him to the cross. It must be that there is a "you" who is the ultimate subject of the treading and who is beyond harm. It might be the "you" that Spanish poet Antonio Machado thought was a core perception of Jesus.

> Christ spoke another truth:
> Find the you that is not yours
> and never can be.[12]

This must be the spiritual center. It has no life of its own, but it is constantly receiving life and love from God. Therefore, it establishes a "you that is not yours."

At the end of the Sermon on the Mount, Jesus tells the crowds and his disciples what the result is of "hearing and doing" the words he has just spoken. They will be like wise men who built their house on rock. The rains fell, the floods came, and the winds blew but the house survived because it was built on rock. This was the same rock that Jesus saw in Peter when Peter recognized him as the Son of the living God. Nothing could prevail against this rock, even the power of hell.

The night-sea journey in the Gospel of John symbolizes a similar teaching (John 6:16–21). There is a storm on the sea of Galilee and the wind and waves threaten the disciples' boat. Jesus comes to them, walking on the tumultuous sea. He tells them, "It is I; do not be afraid." The story abruptly states: "They wanted to receive him into the boat, and immediately the boat reached land." All they had to do was desire to receive him, and through him his self-giving Father, and they were safe. They had a place to stand. This time it was land, but the land conveys the same meaning as rock. The giving and receiving between God and our spiritual center cannot be broken. "The darkness cannot overcome it."

Following

Part of following someone is that we surmise that he or she is farther along the path than we are. We can learn from that person. In the case of Jesus, he is the kingdom of God in himself, the full embodiment of the God–Self–Neighbor spiritual process. In particular, he is the Son of Father, receiving spiritual life that establishes him in a love flow. He can say, "All things have been handed over to me by my Father; and no one knows who the Son is except the Father; or who the Father is except the Son and anyone to whom the Son chooses to reveal him" (Luke 10:22). We are told Jesus said these words "thrilled by the Holy Spirit." I take this to mean he was conscious of the life and love of the Father as he was speaking.

As a follower of Jesus, I am one of those to whom the Son chooses to reveal the Father. I receive this revelation of a dynamic relationship between the self-giving Spirit and the receiving soul. But it is well beyond my consciousness. It is the master's mountaintop; I live in the plain. His garments turn dazzlingly white, and I am overshadowed by a voice that says, "Listen to him" (Mark 9:2–8). So I listen. I take it on faith. But no sooner do I do this then I find out the theological maxim that faith seeks understanding is painfully true. I am driven toward greater understanding. This understanding is wide-ranging. It not only wants to grasp the logic of this divine-human relationship, it also hungers for some personal realization of it. But I am not sure how to go about it.

One exchange between Jesus and Peter suggests we let go of any images and ways of thinking that might divert our attention from the act of receiving (John 13:6–8). When Jesus came to Peter to wash and dry his feet, Peter's sensibilities were affronted. "Lord, do *you* wash *my* feet?" In Peter's mind it is inappropriate for the Lord to be engaged in this task. It should be reversed. Peter should be washing the feet of Jesus. After all, Jesus is the Lord and Peter should be serving him. This is the way superior-inferior relationships work. Subjects serve lords. The rules are clear and right. Peter holds firm, "You will never wash my feet."

Some commentators suspect Peter saw the unfolding logic of what Jesus was doing and tried to short-circuit the process. If he let Jesus, the Lord, wash and dry his feet, then he, the leader, would have to wash and dry the feet of lesser disciples. This chain of service would have disastrous effects on hierarchial privilege. Peter was comfortable playing the traditional version of master-servant, and he did not want to enter into Jesus' reversal dynamics. Jesus forthrightly tells Peter that he does not know what Jesus is doing, and the reason he does not know is his addiction to other metaphors for God.

I suspect Peter is not alone. His resistance lurks in all. The metaphor of foot washing and drying translates into: that which is most powerful is serving us. It is hard to swallow, especially when we have been trained in the school of the Lord of Hosts who makes all nations the footstool under his feet. We can get on board with the Judge of the living and the dead. We all know the sweet fantasy of power that makes others, especially those who have done us wrong, wilt. In fact, when we manage to pull off some outrageous piece of oppression, we are confronted with: "Who do you think you are — God?" Oppressive and ultimately victorious power has market appeal.

Now Jesus is proposing something which, at first glance, appears weaker and more passive. Do we really want to trade the All-Powerful Lord of Heaven and Earth for a servant Spirit who refreshes us for the journey? If we look into our ego, we will see Peter's face and the answer will be no. We will resist because it does not square, and may be the exact opposite, of metaphors that we already hold and that have a strong hold on us. But, if we are ever going to learn to receive, we have to let go of these muscular metaphors, or at least not allow them to completely occupy our minds. We cannot open and receive Spirit when we are waiting for the soldiers of the King to arrive.

Ridding the mind of obstacles is complemented by training it in new abilities. For a while I worked with an esoteric Christian meditation called, "Behold a mystical rose." The ones meditating begin at the top of the rose where the tips of the petals do not touch. At this point they are encouraged to realize the truth of separateness. We live in a world of multiplicity. Then their eyes glide down the rose and rest on the overlapping sections of the petals. This sight encourages consciousness to realize similarities and commonalities among what appeared as separate. When the eyes reach the base of the rose, all the petals come from the same stem. This is the deepest realization of the one source of all things and, therefore, a fundamental communion among all things. I liked this imaginative exercise and I practiced it often. But it strengthened a unitive vision of creation rather than the God-Soul relationship.

I also tried to deepen my interiority by following a general set of instructions for achieving inner unity. We must begin by struggling inwardly, pulling away from everything that would dissipate our mind and will. In technical language, we must withdraw from multiplicity into inner unity. This includes both detaching from the outer world and, as we draw back, taking with us all our powers of body and mind. We integrate these powers into our highest power, the spiritual center that has an open and receiving relationship with the Mystery of Spirit. Once this is accomplished, we form the single-minded intention to be of God and of God's purposes. We disengage from any other desires, especially those that our egos are continually manufacturing. We are now empty and waiting. According to the theory, Spirit cannot resist emptiness. It would fill this virgin-point and make me pregnant. But

I found waiting is not a temporary stance and my emptiness was filled by patience.

The Gift of Myself

As I was pursuing my following of Jesus in this crucial area of learning how to receive, I began to experience "things" as gifts rather than products of my own making or random happenstances. I would have a thought. But to claim I had generated it or that now I possessed it was not true to the dynamics of its actual arrival. It seemed to have come unbidden, a surprising gift more than anything else. I would be at a meeting and someone would say something, and I had to resist the urge to say thank you. It was like the words were meant for my solace. And I started to recognize all the people in life, both close and far, as undeserved gifts. I repented of previously taking them for granted. I even stopped evaluating the weather. It was neither good nor bad. Just given.

This sense of gift awakened gratitude. The gratitude began to spread, rising above particular people and events and becoming an atmosphere. It was a free-floating gratitude for life itself. I was answering the question I posed on the porch. But the thankfulness did not come from the shock of nonbeing. It came from excess, from an abundance of being, filling everything and, seemingly, offering it up to the Source from which it came. I remembered the Gospel of John that started me down this path. "From his fullness, we have all received, grace upon grace" (John 1:16).

But more was brewing. I began to recall and tell aspects of my life story that I had previously overlooked. And every telling seemed to strengthen the same truth. To echo the dying words of the young curate in *Diary of a Country Priest,* "It's all grace."

When I began to speak in public, friends of my parents would often show up. They were not really interested in theology or spirituality, but they were loyal to the clan. After one talk, a man told me, "You have your uncle's body, but you've got your father's way."

I went back to my father and told him, "He said I've got Steve's body, but your way."

My father pondered that for a moment. "I suppose he's right." Then he paused and sighed, "Thank God, you've got your mother's brains."

At the time I was in the throes of some prolonged pain in my legs that evaded diagnosis and treatment. A friend came to see me. I was sitting in a chair with my legs on an ottoman. My muscles were twitching, fasciculations. He asked, "Have they figured out what you've got."

"Not yet," I said, "but it could be poliomyelitis — multiple muscle disease. My father had it."

My friend has a wicked sense of humor. He smiled and pretended to chide me. "Shut up. If you get the brains, you get the legs."

I am not good at quick replies, but I informed him. "The brains are my mother's."

I added it up. I had my uncle's body, my father's way and perhaps his legs, and my mother's brains. Where did I — me, myself, and I — come in? I knew the answer. I had taken all this raw material and whipped it into shape. It was my energy and initiative that was important. I counted my achievements like a miser counting coins.

Then something happened that plunged me irretrievably into the consciousness of gift. I had accepted an invitation to give a storytelling workshop in Ireland. Halfway over the Atlantic, I had an anxiety attack of major proportions. Who did I think I was? Going to Ireland to give a workshop on storytelling was carrying coals to Newcastle.

But the Irish were kind and welcoming to the brash Yank. I gave an evening lecture to the public. Afterward, a man approached and told me he knew the brother of my grandfather. I jumped the gun.

"Tim Shea?" I volunteered.

"Ah, no," the man said. "Jerry Mullarkey. You are the grandson of John Thomas Mullarkey, are you not?"

"Yes, on my mother's side."

"Jerry Mullarkey was a shenacke, a storyteller. Like yourself. He lived on a mountain, and he used to ride his bike down the mountain to tell stories at wakes and weddings."

Later that night I sat on the edge of the bed, and once again pondered my own private chain of being. I had my uncle's body, my father's way and perhaps his legs, my mother's brains; and now it turns out I had my grandfather's brother's psychic structure. For if there would be an imaginative way to say how the physical, social, psychic, and spiritual complex comes together in me, it would be to simply describe me as a man who rides his bicycle down the mountain to tell stories at wakes and weddings. I might have done something with it, but I could no longer ignore that everything was given, from genetic material on up.

But, on the edge of that bed, I received this realization differently. Before, I had felt vaguely diminished by the serious recognition of gift. Now, once I laughingly gave in to it, I felt a rush of liberation and energy. What I felt liberated from was a whole psychological and social superstructure that I had scaffolded around my fragile sense of self. I knew I owned nothing, and this relaxed state of mind allowed me to open to Spirit. As I did, Spirit arrived and I welcomed it. It whispered to me, "I was here from the beginning."

The $10,000 Homily

In the middle 1980s I made ten thousand dollars on a homily. I like to say it that way. It has shock value. I was preaching on the famous lilies of the field passage (Matt. 6:25–34). I stressed that on the surface this passage looked like it was pitting trust in God against prudent financial planning. But I held the passage was really about something else, and I tried to explain what that was. A man in the congregation agreed with me and told me so outside Church after the liturgy. "I always felt that passage was nonsense," he said.

The pastor called me the following week. He told me the man had given ten thousand dollars to the church and ten thousand dollars to me. I was hesitant to accept it. It seemed wrong, and it made me wonder what my homily had played into. The pastor laughed and insisted I take it. He said he had no intention of telling anyone and he didn't care what I did with it. I took it, and started a journal for seminarians — theology, poems, stories, etc. I would be the editor and the journal would pay them to write for it. Ah, incentive! It was ill-fated, but the money did get around and helped some struggling students.

Like the man in the congregation, I had trouble with the lilies of the field. As long as it remained poetic rhapsody, it was beautiful to read and recite. But when I asked if I personally thought or acted like that, the answer was no. The combination of injunctions and questions puzzled me. "Do not worry about your life: what you will eat or what you will drink, or about your body, what you will wear." It seemed clear to me why I worried about these things. I had an inherent drive to survive, a natural desire to persist in being. It was built into me. If I abandoned the worry, existence might abandon me. "Or why do you worry about your clothing?" This was not a concern about style, fretting over high fashion. It was about basic covering to keep from freezing, frying, or being put in jail for indecent exposure.

The offset to these concerns was birds that didn't work, but who nevertheless were fed by "your heavenly Father"; and lilies that likewise did not toil or spin, but yet they manage to outshine Solomon. Therefore, if "your" heavenly father did this for bird and lilies, how much more would he do it for you? This argument, couched in beautiful language, was less than persuasive. Need I mention dead birds on the sidewalks and faded lilies in the field?

We are better at seeing life as perilous and responding in anxiety and worry than we are at seeing life as a gift and responding with gratitude.

It took me awhile to recognize that my gut reaction against this poetic argument was its point. I was so into worry, so into seeing my life as an anxious project of survival that I was on the verge of frenzy if anything else was suggested. It is this confinement of consciousness that rejects gift consciousness in principle. We cannot let go of our fear and worry lest tomorrow bring our extinction. When the passage ends with, "So do not worry about tomorrow for tomorrow will worry about itself," we might laugh; and with the laugh the tough hide of survival opens and gift and gratitude become a possibility.

Right now, in this very moment, there is an option. We can look at our lives as an anxious project of survival, a series of never-ending worries; or we can look at our lives as free gifts sustained in mysterious ways as birds are fed by the earth and lilies grow without work. Both options have truth in them. One is not false and the other true; and both must live together. But the fact is that we are better at seeing life as perilous and responding in anxiety and worry than we are at seeing life as a gift and responding with gratitude. The issue is what killed the conversation on the porch — ontological gratitude.

When we open to sheer giftedness, it is quite amazing. We fill up from within and spill over. Caught in the ever deepening consciousness of gratitude, we say stupid, unpractical things like the gift of life and connection with the source who continually gives is enough. We nod as if we agree with Habakkuk.

> Though the fig tree does not blossom,
>   and no fruit is on the vine;
> though the produce of the olive fails,
>   and the fields yield no food;
> though the flock is cut off from the fold,
>   and there is no herd in the stalls;
>   yet I will rejoice in the Lord.
>   —Habakkuk 3:17–18

When we are filled with gift consciousness, we are tempted to take a piece of bread like it was our embodied life and give thanks. The burning heart knows this temptation and gives into it whenever it can.

Where We Are

At the baptism of Jesus, the heavens opened, the Spirit descended as a dove, and a voice confided, "You are my beloved Son in whom I am well pleased" (Luke 3:21–22). Some commentators call the ripped heavens a "gracious gash." It established the consciousness of God's free gift of love to Jesus and revealed his ultimate identity as the Son of God, a relational flow between himself and God. However, this is not unique to Jesus. What Jesus knew in himself, he saw in others. And he tried to reveal this amazing truth to his followers in a way they could discover it for themselves and awaken to divine love at the core of their being.

There are many obstacles to this consciousness, but all of them can be surmounted. Also, although everyone's path will be different, everyone must be on the path. The reason is that only the beloved Sons and Daughters know what "well pleased" means. When we receive God's indestructible life, we immediately coincide with the pleasure of reconciling the world to its Source and all people to each other. This is the mission of those who have received their life as a gift and given thanks. They must continue the following and learn how to break and give.

My family, decently large, was gathered at my parents' house. It was our custom to let the youngest say grace. This was not any formulaic recital. It was spontaneous and could go on so long that preempting "Amens" tried to stop it. However, this night as we sat down at the table, my father said,

"I'll say grace." This was unprecedented. There was immediate silence, and we all bowed our heads and looked at our
empty plates. Nothing was coming, no words from our father.
Finally, I looked up from my plate to see what the delay was.
Our father's head was slightly tilted upward, his mouth was
agape, his eyes were opened, and two streams of tears flowed
down his cheeks. Finally, the choked words came, "Thank
you!" He was thrilled by the Holy Spirit. And so was his son.

Chapter Eight _____

Neighbor: Breaking and Giving

S R. MARGIE TUITE was a friend and a lifelong advocate for civil rights and women's equality, especially poor women. She loved to tell a story about a talk she gave to a group of women. Margie drew stick figures on the board that represented various styles of relationship. One pair of figures was grossly mismatched. The first one towered above the second and glared down at it. Although it was a simple drawing, it expressed a world that many women knew only too well. After the talk a woman who did not speak English came up to Margie and pounded on the board, hitting the lower figure with her fist and shouting, "Me! Me! Me!"

I was in a small group where Margie told that story. One of the members said something to the effect of: "Well and good. But what if she gets out of the relationship. Where will she go? What will she do?"

Margie was on the edge of her chair. Her arms were out in front of her, her hands parallel to each other, like they were gripping some large object. I suspect the man's head. She was about to attack, but she didn't. Instead, she slid back into the chair, did not talk for a moment, and then in a tired

115

voice spelled out to all of us what was so obvious to her. I don't remember her exact words, but I cannot forget her drift. "Whenever there is suffering and domination, you break it. Sure you find yourself out in the dark. The problem is you've gotten used to sin; you've gotten comfortable being a slave. Oppression is a habit. Whether you are on the top or the bottom, you're part of it. And part of breaking it is finding yourself in unfamiliar territory, not knowing what to do next."

A Law of the Spirit

There are laws and operations in every dimension of life. The universe, our physical bodies, the social constructions we live within, and the mental processes that churn on and on work in certain ways. Some of these ways we call "ironclad laws," especially in the cosmic and bodily dimensions. Other ways we say are predictable dynamics that we ignore at our own cost, especially in the social and mental arenas. But all these ways should be heeded, even obeyed. We may be free, but we are not absolutely free. Human nature is under constraints; and if we are going to flourish, we have to move in harness.

There is a particularly scary law of the spiritual dimension, one that Jesus presses upon his followers. It is on display in several of his parables and wisdom sayings. There was a king who had a servant who owed him a tremendous debt (Matt. 18:23–35). He had compassion on the servant and

forgave him. But the servant went out and found and throt-
tled a fellow servant who owed him a paltry debt. When the
king found out, he called the first servant to him. "I forgave
you all that debt because you pleaded with me. . . . Should you
not have had mercy on your fellow servant as I had mercy on
you?" Then the king handed him over to the torturers until
he paid his entire debt. The moral is: what you have received
you should give; if you do not, what you have received will be
taken from you. This law is also succinctly stated in the Lord's
Prayer. "Forgive us our trespasses as we forgive those who
trespass against us" (Matt. 6:12). There is no use pleading
extenuating circumstances in an effort to keep the forgiveness
of God when you have refused forgiveness to your neighbor.
Spiritual laws run their course.

*Oppression is a habit. Whether you
are on the top or the bottom, you're
part of it. And part of breaking
it is finding yourself in unfamiliar
territory, not knowing what to
do next.*

But there is a positive side to this spiritual law. If we give to
others what we have received from the Mystery of Spirit, we
receive even more from the Mystery. A man who was going
away called three of his servants and gave them differing sums
of money — ten talents, five talents, and one talent (Matt.

25:14–30). During the time the man was gone, the first two servants doubled what they had received, making ten and five talents more. The man tells them to "enter into the joy of their master." They have given as they have received, and what they have received has increased. Now they understand in a whole new way the *joy* of their master. When Spirit that is received is not given away, it is taken away. When Spirit that is received is given way, it is increased. Once again, wanting it otherwise is futile. This is just how Spirit works.

Therefore, it is essential for Spirit-infused heavenly consciousness to come to earth if it is to be preserved and developed. The underlying reason for this law is the nature of Spirit itself. It is essentially self-giving; so when it is received, it merges its nature with the ones who receive it. If they try to possess it, they work against its inherent dynamism and find they lose it. When they give it away, they become one with it, and they inherit everlasting life. Eternal life is the endless receiving, thanking, breaking, and giving that goes on in the God–Self–Neighbor spiritual process.

The Struggle

However, there are major discrepancies between heavenly consciousness and earthly realities. In heavenly consciousness, we realize the Mystery of Spirit pours life and love into us to such a degree that we are sons and daughters of Spirit. This fundamental realization has important implications. We come to see our child of God identity is the hidden truth of all people. Therefore, since all are "sons and daughters of their Father in heaven," we should live as brothers and sisters with one another, bearing each other's burdens. These notions of universal human dignity and social harmony are not ideals to be achieved, as if they existed nowhere. They are the truth of the spiritual dimension.

But universal human dignity and social harmony are not prevalent on earth. On earth the default mode is inequality and division. People are respected only if they have the position and power to command it. There are enmities between families, ethnic groups, and races. The rich have no concern for the poor. A rich man can feast sumptuously while the beggar at his door starves and dogs lick his wounds (Luke 16:20). Therefore, when those with heavenly consciousness enter this world of alienation, they are the light of this world and the salt of this earth (Matt. 5:13–16). Their light exposes these estranged relationships and shows another way. Their salt brings zest and joy to what is without life and happiness. However, their behavior calls attention to itself because they are not conforming to the expected cultural conditions of alienation. This heightens the contrast. "For as the heavens are higher than the earth, so are my ways higher than your ways, [says the Lord]" (Isa. 55:9).

Jesus lives on this border of heaven and earth, and so he is acutely aware of this tension and its challenges. Paul Tillich described Jesus as essential God-Manhood under the conditions of existence. He was the union of the divine and human in a world where the divine and human were separated. He lived unity under the conditions of disunity. His heavenly consciousness confronted the consciousness and behavior of the earth. In a word, Jesus didn't fit; and his non-fit became the relentless energy of transformation.

Most significantly, Jesus did not respect the social boundaries that earthly societies establish and protect. He reached out to everyone — children, women and men, the sick, the unclean, demoniacs, tax collectors, Gentiles, sinners, etc. This was because he saw in everyone what he knew in himself. He saw a daughter of Abraham in a stooped over woman and a son of Abraham in a small tax collector (Luke 13:16; 19:1–10). Dag Hammarskjöld certainly has Jesus right.

> Jesus' "lack of moral principles." He sat at meat with publicans and sinners, he consorted with harlots. Did he do this to obtain their votes? Or did he think that, perhaps, he could convert them by such "appeasement"? Or was his humanity rich and deep enough to make contact, even in them, with what in human nature is common to all men, indestructible, and upon which the future has to be built?[13]

This common identity translates into a common community. People who had been pushed out or who had walked out should be welcomed back. In order to achieve this, forgiveness becomes a central strategy because it is only through forgiveness that reconciliation will happen. This drive to inclusivity is imaged as a shepherd who is not satisfied with ninety-nine sheep but looks for the one who is lost, or as a woman with nine coins ardently seeking the missing tenth, or as a father holding together two sons who have been alienated from him and each other (Luke 15:1–32). However, this unitive way of heaven is not welcomed on the divisive earth. "The Pharisees went out and immediately conspired with the Herodians against him, how to destroy him" (Mark 3:6).

The Kingdom and the Cross

Many years ago I was in a priest reflection group. I do not remember the topic under discussion. But, out of nowhere, one of the priests said, looking at the floor, "I continually ask forgiveness for some of the advice I gave in the confessional." The group went quiet. Then someone asked, "What do you mean?" He looked up. "I told people to carry their crosses when I should have told them to make changes or get out."

In the Catholic world of the immediate past "carrying your cross" was an all-purpose response to every suffering. If you had a serious illness, or if you were living with an abusive spouse, or if you were alienated from a family member, or if you could not afford another child but could not refrain from sex, or if you were saddled with an oppressive obligation, the advice was predictable: "We all have crosses. You have to carry yours." Sometimes an attempt at consolation and encouragement was added. "God won't give you more than you can bear."

However, in the following of Jesus the cross is a very specific social response to his consciousness and behavior, and "carrying your cross" is a very specific counter-response. In the Gospels Jesus' heavenly consciousness and corresponding earthly behavior are suspect from the beginning. His way of dignity and communion is at odds with those invested in privilege and division. These people are in positions of religious and political authority — Pharisees, Sadducees, Herodians, and a Roman procurator in the Gospels. They are not about to look the other way while Jesus is trying to reorganize their kingdoms as the Kingdom of God. They have power, and how they use it, complete with lies and rationalizations, results in the arrest, trial, and execution of Jesus.

Is this just the response of Jesus' culture and society? Or will heavenly consciousness and its corresponding earthly behavior always meet with persecution? If followers of Jesus try to bring heaven to earth, will their families think them out of their minds (Mark 3:21)? Will communities beg them to leave (Mark 6:17). Will religious and political leaders plot against them and threaten anyone they love and care about (John 12:10)? It has been known to happen, and many think it is absolutely predictable.

The kingdom of God will always be at odds with the kingdoms of the world. The temptation narratives make this clear (Luke 4:1–13). Satan owns the kingdoms of the world, and he offers them to Jesus. The price is that Jesus has to worship the *diabolus,* the one who divides, and the *Satanas,* the one who accuses. However, Jesus is already committed to the opposite dynamics of forgiveness and reconciliation. So he refuses. This conflict, this not going along with the way of the world, leads to persecution. Count on it. The cross is the symbol that the spiritual dimension and the social dimension will never be completely aligned.

Followers are not reluctant victims, submitting to persecution. They take on and transform hostility. They take up their cross and carry it.

If that is the case, followers of Jesus must be prepared to respond to the persecution they will encounter. "If any want to be my followers, let them deny themselves and take up their cross and follow me" (Matt. 16:24). On one level, the cross is imposed on followers by those who violently oppose the Kingdom. "From the days of John the Baptist until now the Kingdom of heaven has suffered violence, and the violent bear it away" (Matt. 11:12). However, what is put on followers by force, they must proactively take up. Followers are not reluctant victims, submitting to persecution. They take on and transform hostility. They take up their cross and carry it.

This response of "carrying your cross" fascinated a teenage high school student commenting on the traditional second station of the cross, *Jesus takes up his cross.*

Whenever I disagreed with my second-year religion teacher, Mrs. Kurtz (which was often), she'd always say, "Well, Jeffrey, how do you see it?"

Well, this is how I see it.

Jesus was no dummy. He saw the cross coming. Look at what he was doing! He's touching all the unclean people, eating with outcasts, breaking up the temple money game, criticizing corruption. He wants a better world, but a lot of people are doing real well in the world as it is. They are not going to give up and fade away. This is not news.

Now Peter — there's a dummy. Jesus lays it out for him — the cross, the resurrection, the whole thing — and he says, "No way."

Jesus is not happy.

So Jesus says to him, "Not only for me, but for you too, Peter."

So now Peter is not happy.

So Jesus tells him — and here's the thing I like — Jesus tells him, "Don't let them lay the cross on you, Peter. Take it up. Don't' let them lay it on you. Take it up."

Wow! You gotta love Jesus for that.

So, Mrs. Kurtz, that's how Jeffrey sees it.[14]

The classic expression of this assertive attitude is the final beatitude. "Blessed are you when people revile you and persecute you and utter all kinds of evil against you falsely on my account. Rejoice and be glad, for your reward is great in heaven, for in the same way they persecuted the prophets who were before you" (Matt. 5:11).

"Taking up our cross" is a matter of fidelity to heavenly consciousness in an earthly setting. When persecution arrives, we can walk away and give up the project of following Jesus. Or we can fight persecutors in the same way as they are fighting us, the way of retaliation, an eye for an eye and a tooth for a tooth. Or we can treat our persecutors with heavenly consciousness and behavior. "Love your enemies, do good to those who hate you, bless those who curse you, pray for those who abuse you" (Luke 6:27). Even though this response opens followers to the ill will of their persecutors, it is consistent with heavenly consciousness and witnesses to the conviction that God's way will ultimately transform the earth. It is why throughout Christian history there has been a strong link between discipleship and martyrdom.

The Kingdom and the Yoke

It was around two o'clock on a Sunday afternoon in late September of 1967. I had just finished closing the church and was eating lunch when the phone rang. The caller identified himself and told me the situation. "My wife has locked herself in the car in the driveway and she won't come out. Can you come over here and help me?"

It was a hot day and the woman in the back seat was perspiring. She was also cringing, her arms wrapped around herself. I shouted through the window, "Why won't you come out?" She cried, but didn't say anything. I asked her husband. He shrugged.

In those days the problem of domestic abuse was not as well known as it is today. But I suspected this was not a crazy woman but a very scared woman. I stood there awhile, and then tried again. "Do you have a friend or relative in the area?" She nodded.

The husband picked it up. "She has a sister close by."

"Call her," I told him.

"We don't need her."

"Call her," I said again.

When the sister arrived, the wife unlocked the door and got out on the side away from her husband. The sister hugged her around the shoulders, stared at the husband and me, but said nothing. She walked her sister to her car.

A couple of days later, I called the husband. His wife was back home. I gave him the telephone number of Catholic Charities. I strongly urged him to call.

In January of 1968, I enrolled in Loyola's psychology program to get an M.A. in counseling. I had to get better.

Although there can be preparation, there are no scripts for the next moment. They are written as each incredibly detailed situation unfolds.

Followers of Jesus may meet the cross that always waits. But they also may meet the yoke that always waits. The yoke is the discipline to learn the ways of the earth with enough discernment and skill to change them for the better. We have stressed the need to begin with receiving and thanking God as the deathless energy of all life's projects. The plus of this approach is that we know something more than the situations we find ourselves in. So we are less likely to conform to them, especially if the situation is marked by alienation and division. The minus of this approach is it does not tell us what respecting human dignity and pursuing reconciliation looks like in diverse situations. Being on the "side of the angels" is a real detriment when we do not know how to be on "the side of people."

Therefore, followers must master the ways of earth in order to bring heaven into it. They have to become excellent in politics, law, economics, education, healthcare, banking, business, etc. But even with expertise, the intractable particularity of each situation awaits. Each day we enter the adventure of the unforeseen. Our consciousness must be rooted in heaven and alert to the ways of earth. Although there can be preparation, there are no scripts for the next moment. They are written as each incredibly detailed situation unfolds. What do I do with a woman locked in a car?

Ever new situations mean that first actions will never be perfect or complete. When we notice our contribution did not work out as we intended, we enter more completely into the struggle of bringing heaven to earth and embrace a key attitude in the following of Jesus — repentance. Repentance is redoing situations until they reflect as best they can human dignity and reconciliation. Repentance is not what bad people have to do. It is what people who live out of transcendent values find necessary. Also, repentance is not a one-time thing or a fallback that is done only as necessary. It is the pervading atmosphere of attempts to bring the Kingdom. Repenting is forever.

Where We Are

Followers want to be the good earth that receives the seed and manages to produce a hundredfold (Luke 8:4–15). The way to abundant harvest is clearly spelled out. The seed that is the Word must be "held fast in a good and generous heart." When we hold it fast, we do not allow it to be pushed aside by other concerns. The Word becomes an unwavering structure of consciousness. It is grounded in the goodness of the heart, which means it is grounded in the goodness of God, which the heart receives. Receiving the goodness of God, which is diffusive of itself, immediately translates into generosity. We act in the world in such a way that people will "see our good works and give glory to our Father in heaven" (Matt. 5:16). The Source of human action will be acknowledged.

But, according to Jesus' interpretation of the parable, bringing forth a hundredfold will be accomplished only through "patient endurance." Our minds want quick solutions. We can run the hundred-yard dash but not the lifelong marathon. Like receiving and thanking, breaking and giving is forever activity. Followers must be patient and they must endure. The message is: settle in, don't look for it to be over, relax, stay faithful. This is what it is.

Margie called me one night from Manhattan to tell me she was going to have an operation for cancer in the morning. As we talked, she said, "I've angered a lot of people, but I stayed faithful." She did not survive the operation.

There was a woman, a widow with no connections or power, and she kept coming to a judge, saying, "Grant me justice." But the judge refused. Still she kept coming. Finally, the judge said to himself, "I fear neither God nor man. But this woman won't let go. I will give her justice because she is wearing me out" (Luke 18:1–8).

Chapter Nine

Wagering on Resurrection

WE WAKE BEFORE our spouse and children. We ramble toward the kitchen to get breakfast going. The cat is underfoot, looking for water and food. We put the coffee on and take a piece of paper from a cabinet. On it is a Gospel passage we typed out over a week ago. This is our fourth day of reading and thinking about it.

Jesus has told a story to some religious elites about two sons and their father (Matt. 21:28–32). The father told both to work in the field. One said yes and didn't do it. The other said no, then thought better of it, and did it. Jesus wants to know which one did the will of the father. We know the answer, but the answer does not seem important.

The first son has captured our attention. He smiled yes, but he acted no. We mollify people with promises we think will make them happy. We get comfortable with gaps between our thoughts and our speech. We are always hiding from full disclosure, maximizing our advantage. Transparency is a joke. Suddenly a family situation rises in our memory. Then the beeper on the coffee machine goes off. The day stretches before us. It is carefully planned, but within the structure of our schedule we have no idea what will happen.

Looking for Jesus

By all accounts the crucifixion of Jesus was a dream-crushing event for the disciples. We immediately resonate. If we live long enough, and it doesn't have to be that long, we understand the fragility of hope, especially when that hope is tied to someone who dies. "We had hoped that he was the one to redeem Israel" (Luke 24:21). With the disciples sunk in despair and grief, we naturally assume the resurrection pulled them out of it. It was a joyous reversal, the return of the one who was lost and with him the reestablishment of their dream. Years of watching Hollywood movies has an effect.

But, on the whole, the Gospels portray the resurrection as disconcerting, extending the disruption of expectations that the arrest, trial, and execution began. In the first moment, the resurrection does not mean Jesus was found after being lost. Rather, if the narrative plot is honored, it means that Jesus could not be found. He was not where those who die are supposed to be. He was not in the tomb.

In the Gospel of Luke, the women inside the empty tomb are startled to suddenly find two men in dazzling clothes. "They were terrified and bowed their faces to the ground" (Luke 24:5). But the two men may have been equally startled. Their question, "Why do you look for the living among the dead?" suggests they are surprised to see the women in this place of emptiness. If they are looking for Jesus, they should be elsewhere.

A similar situation is portrayed in the other Gospels. The women in Matthew suffer an earthquake and a descending angel who rolls back the stone at the entrance of the tomb, sits on it, and tells them, "I know you are looking for Jesus of Nazareth who was crucified. He is not here" (Matt. 28:5). In Mark, the women are inside the tomb when a young man in a white robe informs them, "You are looking for Jesus of Nazareth who was crucified.... He is not here" (Mark 16:6). In John, Mary Magdalene finds out for herself that the Lord is not in the tomb where she thought he would be (John 20:1–2). The followers of Jesus are following the cultural protocol of going to the tomb to anoint the dead, but they are discovering that in the case of Jesus they are in the wrong place.

It is an understandable mistake. Although tombs contain only remains, we conventionally identify body and person so completely that we follow the body in hopes of finding the person. "Visiting graves" has a long and respectable history and, I believe, its deepest motivation is the gut instinct that we can still be in contact with those who have died. We do not let go of what we love easily; and what we have loved for so long is embodied persons. In the past when we wanted to see them, we journeyed to where they were and entered into conversation. Common sense determined absence and presence. When we could physically see and hear them, we were in their presence. When we could not physically see and hear them, we were absent from them. We grasp this way of physical presence in our gut. That is why we go to where the body is, even if the full person as we knew him or her will not be there. That is also why the picture of Mary Magdalene weeping outside the tomb because she cannot find Jesus' body touches us so deeply (John 20:11).

Although tombs contain only remains, we conventionally identify body and person so completely that we follow the body in hopes of finding the person.

However, in the Gospels there is also the implication the women should have known better. During his life Jesus had predicted not only his handing over and death but also his resurrection. "Then he began to teach them that the Son of Man must undergo great suffering, and be rejected by the elders, the chief priests, and the scribes, and be killed, and after three days rise again" (Mark 8:31). Despite the predictions the disciples are unprepared for these events and react badly when they occur. They betray, deny, and abandon Jesus during his arrest, trial, and execution; and they go to the tomb even though "rise from dead" would indicate that he would not be there. Jesus' predictions may have been heard, but they were not comprehended to the degree that they changed the accustomed way of behaving.

The disciples' inability to understand "rising from the dead" and their failure to remember it when they should have is significant. We are not dealing with dense people who suffered a memory lapse. Jesus did not give them a peek into the future that they forgot when the predicted future actually started to unfold. The predictions are not an informational checklist — hand over, suffer, die, and rise.

They are symbolic statements, profound teachings expressing a radical change of consciousness. As such, they do not immediately replace the conventional consciousness that has long been assumed and taken for granted. Instead, the predictions are heard as discordant, as not making immediate sense, as a puzzle that needs further clarification. The disciples' confusion with the whole process of death and resurrection is the labor pains of a new consciousness. After one of the predictions, the disciples "question what this rising from the dead could mean" (Mark 9:10).

With close to two thousand years of reflection on the event of Jesus Christ, we think we know what this rising from the dead means. Resurrection is the first step of an exaltation process. The risen Lord ascends into heaven and sits at the right hand of the Father. From this position where "all authority on heaven and earth" has been given to him, he sends the Spirit, who enlivens his followers to continue his mission of preaching, teaching, and living the Good News (Matt. 28:18). This has been the plan from the beginning of Jesus' life. He knew this plan and he obediently lived it out. But it was hidden from his followers until after the resurrection. Now that they are privy to the plan, Jesus' location is known and their mission confirmed. However, this encapsulation of Jesus' destiny may overlook dynamics that are important to following him, to grasping death and resurrection not as a series of events but as a frightening yet real vision of reality.

Finding Jesus

If Jesus is not in the tomb, where is he?

The beginning of an answer is that he is in Galilee, going ahead of his disciples, and there they will see him. This is what the young man in white (Mark 16:7), the angel (Matt. 28:7), and even Jesus himself (Matt. 28:10) tell the women to convey to "his [Jesus'] brothers." In fact, the risen Lord himself gives a more specific destination than the general region of Galilee. He directs his brothers to a *mountain* in Galilee where they will see him (Matt. 28:16). This is the mountain where he was seated, with his disciples close to him, and taught the crowds at length. At that time he summarized his teachings in a monologue that became the legendary Sermon on the Mount (Matt. 5:1–7:28).

These directions to the mountain in Galilee are not geographical. They are symbolic code for how the disciples will see him. They alert them to the new conditions of Jesus' presence. As they live out the teachings of the Sermon on the Mount, they will see Jesus in his risen state. The fact that he is already in Galilee and going ahead of them reinforces his permanent leadership. No one will replace Jesus as the head of his community of disciples. Also, his "going ahead" means the following continues. As they struggle to live out his way of life, he will continue to teach them. The teacher-disciple dynamics that were operative as they followed Jesus during his life are still in place. But, of course, these dynamics will go on in a much different way.

The core of this different way is the changed form of Jesus' presence. The disciples will not see him in the way they saw him before his death. Resurrection is not resuscitation. In fact, the risen Lord explicitly tells Mary Magdalene not to cling to the past form of his presence (John 20:17). The changed form is indicated in the resurrection stories. Even though doors are shut, Jesus suddenly appears in the midst of the disciples (John 20:19–29). He walks with two of them who do not recognize him; and then when he breaks bread with them, they recognize him and he vanishes (Luke 24:13–35). The risen Lord can appear and disappear suddenly; his disciples cannot recognize him and then recognize him. Whatever this new form of his presence is, it is not the same as the pre-death presence.

The Gospel of John deals extensively with the simultaneous loss of Jesus in one way and his presence in another way. Jesus comes from the Father into world, accomplishes his mission, and returns to the Father. Therefore, his earthly life, like all our lives, has a discernible beginning and end. But, as he approaches the end of his incarnate life, Jesus tells his disciples he will not leave them orphans. The Father and Son will provide "another paraclete" (John 14:16), a companion and advocate. The implication is that Jesus is the first paraclete and the Holy Spirit is his successor, the second paraclete. The Holy Spirit will function in the same way Jesus has functioned and so provide continuity between the incarnate Jesus and the risen Lord.

> *Our following of Jesus is not loyalty to a past master; it is staying awake and cooperating with his Spirit who beckons in the next never-before-seen-in-the-world moment.*

This continuity between Jesus and the Holy Spirit is emphasized by calling the Holy Spirit "the Spirit of truth" who will guide the disciples into all truth because [he] will take what is Jesus' and declare it to them (John 16:12–13). Also, the "Advocate, the Holy Spirit, whom the Father will send in my name, will teach you everything, and remind you of all that I have said to you" (John 14:26). The Holy Spirit will help the disciples remember and understand what Jesus taught. They already have a record of his words and deeds but "an understanding and remembering" that is a new form of presence will come to them. The first paraclete, Jesus, brought them into a wonderful yet strange consciousness that they could not completely understand. The second paraclete, the Holy Spirit, will bring them into the fullness of this consciousness. This is the basis for Jesus' startling prediction. "Very truly, I tell you, the one who believes in me will also do the works that I do and, in fact, will do greater works than these because I am going to the Father" (John 14:12).

The Wager

If Jesus is not in the tomb, where is he?

He is ahead of us, waiting in every situation as a spiritual presence. This presence calls us to join him in making those situations all they can be. Of course, this call has to be discerned. It arises in and through all the voices that seek to influence every situation. We can "see and hear" him because we have studied and meditated on his life; and he is doing now what he did then. The first and second paracletes are partners. Therefore, our prayer-time is preparation for day-time. The day will unfold and we will have "eyes and ears" for the false notes, the lack of integrity, the failure to align the inside and the outside as a son who told his father he would work in the field and had no intention of doing it. In this way, our following of Jesus is not loyalty to a past master; it is staying awake and cooperating with his Spirit who beckons in the next never-before-seen-in-the-world moment.

Therefore, wagering on resurrection is not betting on an afterlife. It is betting "he is with us always" (Matt. 28:20). This is the new consciousness the first followers were struggling with, the consciousness that could be born only if the conventional consciousness died. But the conventional consciousness regarding life and death does not give way easily.

We might be able to imagine death and resurrection, but we will realize its truthfulness only if we risk enacting it. We must both know and do the God–Self–Neighbor spiritual process.

We must go to Galilee and learn his teachings as tools of discernment. Then we will meet him in situation after situation. He will be ahead of us and we will walk behind. Our amazement will override our knowledge; our fear will battle our courage. It will be like it was in the beginning. "They were on the road, going up to Jerusalem, and Jesus was walking ahead of them; they were amazed and those who followed were afraid" (Mark 10:32).

Notes

1. *Catechism of the Catholic Church* (New York: Doubleday, 1995), 127.

2. For a fuller interpretation of this text, see John Shea, *The Spiritual Wisdom of the Gospels for Christian Preachers and Teachers: On Earth as It Is in Heaven,* Year A: Matthew (Collegeville, Minn.: Liturgical Press, 2004), 246–51.

3. I often type out words that have made an impression on me and then read them slowly so I can more fully grasp their meaning. Since I do this for my own growth, I often do not type out the reference for the quotation, which is the case for this keen observation from Bonhoeffer.

4. For a fuller interpretation of this passage, see John Shea, *The Spiritual Wisdom of the Gospels for Christian Preachers and Teachers: The Relentless Widow,* Year C: Luke (Collegeville, Minn.: Liturgical Press, 2006), 194–200. For a dramatic and expanded retelling of the lawyer's encounter with Jesus, see John Shea, *An Experience of Spirit: Spirituality and Storytelling* (Liguori, Mo.: Liguori Publications, 2004), 156–65.

5. For a fuller interpretation, see John Shea, *The Spiritual Wisdom of the Gospels for Christian Preachers and Teachers: Feasts, Funerals, and Weddings* (Collegeville, Minn.: Liturgical Press, 2009), Palm Sunday, Year C.

6. Cyprian Smith, *The Way of Paradox* (Mahwah, N.J.: Paulist Press, 1987).

7. Walter Wink, *Naming the Powers* (Minneapolis: Fortress Press, 1984), 119, 121.

8. John Haught, *God after Darwin: A Theology of Evolution* (Boulder, Colo.: Westview Press, 2000), 121–22.

9. Rachel Naomi Remen, *Kitchen Table Wisdom* (New York: Riverhead Books, 1996), 78–80.

10. For a fuller interpretation, see John Shea, *Gospel Light: Jesus Stories for Spiritual Consciousness* (New York: Crossroad, 1997), 162–87, and *The Spiritual Wisdom of the Gospels for Christian Preachers and Teachers,* Year A, 166–76.

11. Kallistos Ware, "How Do We Enter the Heart?" in *Paths to the Heart: Sufism and the Christian East* (Bloomington, Ind.: World Wisdom, 2002), 9–11.

12. Antonio Machado, *Selected Poems* (Cambridge, Mass.: Harvard University Press, 1982), 187.

13. Dag Hammarskjöld, *Markings* (New York: Alfred A. Knopf, 1964), 157.

14. John Shea, *Stopping along the Way* (Franklin Park, Ill.: World Library Publications, 2004).

"Truly a spirituality for the 21st century!"
— Dolores Leckey

Catholic Spirituality for Adults

General Editor
Michael Leach

To learn more about forthcoming titles in the series, go to *orbisbooks.com.*

For free study guides and discussion ideas on this book, go to *www.rclbenziger.com.*

Please support your local bookstore.

Thank you for reading *Following Jesus* by John Shea. We hope you found it beneficial.